21st Century
PROPHET

*Second Edition -
Expanded and Updated
Including Worksheets*

SHEENA RYAN

Order this book online at www.trafford.com
or email orders@trafford.com

Most Trafford titles are also available at major online book retailers.

© Copyright 2013 Sheena Ryan.
All rights reserved. No part of this publication may be reproduced, stored in a retrieval system, or transmitted, in any form or by any means, electronic, mechanical, photocopying, recording, or otherwise, without the written prior permission of the author.

Printed in the United States of America.

ISBN: 978-1-4669-8412-7 (sc)
ISBN: 978-1-4669-8414-1 (hc)
ISBN: 978-1-4669-8413-4 (e)

Library of Congress Control Number: 2013904155

Trafford rev. 03/06/2013

 www.trafford.com

North America & international
toll-free: 1 888 232 4444 (USA & Canada)
phone: 250 383 6864 ♦ fax: 812 355 4082

DEDICATION

Thank you to the pastors who believed in me
And released my gift to grow—Pastors Ron and
Leighanne Lay, Pastors Peter and Jan Campbell,
Pastors Chas and Fran Gullo

ENDORSEMENTS

Twenty-First-Century Prophet is a timely and riveting book. My heart was stirred afresh as I read it.

Thanks, Sheena, for sharing these life-changing and powerful truths concerning the prophet's walk. The chapter "The Prophet and the Church" especially is an important message for this hour. I highly recommend this book for this chapter alone!

Sheena models an exemplary way in which a prophet walks in accountability at a local church level and has been an incredible blessing for the team at Suncoast Church.

Twenty-First-Century Prophet is a well-balanced, down-to-earth manual for prophets and prophetic people with lots of real-life examples and outstanding biblical revelation. I love it!

Sheena has done a great job explaining in very practical terms the calling, training, and spiritual life of a New Testament prophet. A must-read for all emerging prophets who have a sincere desire to be used mightily by God!

Fran Gullo
Senior Pastor
Suncoast Christian Church
Cnr Kiel Mtn and Schubert Roads Woombye, Queensland, Australia

Sheena Ryan is a shining flower of the Lord's glory, a gift to the nations. Her patient waiting on the Lord has borne fruit in many lives, even nations. The depth of her prophetic revelations are amazing. Time and again, my wife and I have been truly blessed with Sheena's uncanny and heavenly deliveries of heaven's bread at just the right, strategic time. What a delight to hear her heart poured out in sacrificial harmony from the throne room of God. I would highly recommend this book; it will greatly assist and encourage the reader who desires to know more about the prophetic processes.

Jorge Parrott
Morning Star Ministries Mission Director
Morning Star University College of Theology Director

Preface

Dear Reader,

This book was originally written for those who are called to walk as a fivefold prophet and those who know or minister with a fivefold prophet. I found that so many people of various ages and callings were blessed by it that I have now enlarged the content and would like to say that its application is far more widespread than I could have imagined.

For all those who seek to know more of God's ways and to grow in them, be blessed as you read this.

I use the title of prophet, because it is the title God uses in both the Old and New Testaments. I do not, however, use it in a sense of pride or "better than others" mentality. All spiritual gifts and offices are gifts given to us by God to bless others and are not a badge of honor or favor. By his grace we are what we are.

If this title does not fit your culture or personal conviction, please don't let my use of it deter you from finding any nuggets that may be in this book for you.

I also use the term "prophet" to apply to both men and women. As a woman with this mantle, I believe that the gifts of both men and women have equal value and authority in God's eyes and use the word prophet for convenience. I am speaking of both men and women every time I use it.

I realize also that some of the statements I have made about the process of the prophet relate to people with other gifts as well. I am commenting about these processes, however, in relation to the intensity of training that the prophet receives.

This book contains small excerpts from my life and experiences, as I am often asked how God brought me to the place I am in today. May they encourage you that truly God can and will use anyone who dedicates themselves to his purposes.

Your walk will be individual, but I hope and pray that you will find encouragement, comfort, understanding, and the courage to continue from this book.

Also by Sheena Ryan: *Pathways to Destiny*—Euro Destiny Image

Contents

Introduction xiii

Part I: The Prophet's Pathway to Maturity

Chapter 1	The Distinctives of a Prophet 3
Chapter 2	The Prophet's Pain and Process 26
Chapter 3	The Prophet's Personal War 46
Chapter 4	The Prophet's Impact and Influence 59
Chapter 5	Separating Truth and Error 67
Chapter 6	The Prophet's Maturity and Transition 78
Chapter 7	The Prophet and the Church 97
Chapter 8	Women and Prophetic Mantles 113

Part II: The Battle Manual for Prophetic Warriors

Chapter 1	Removing the Arrows and Shaping the Armor ... 125
Chapter 2	The Forming of a Warrior 131
Chapter 3	Know Your Authority 137
Chapter 4	Know Your Enemy 148
Chapter 5	Gremlins in the Church 151
Chapter 6	Identify Your Battleground 160
Chapter 7	Manifestations of Intercession 166
Chapter 8	Watchmen and Gatekeepers 172

Introduction

This book is an overview of a very profound subject and one which has sometimes been controversial. The prophetic is part of God's end-time plan for his bride, and he desires to put the spotlight on it at this time. If read with a heart open to the spirit of God, this book will bring light and understanding to your pathway and empower you to a fresh passion for the presence of God.

All scriptures are New King James Version unless otherwise specified. Some scriptures I have quoted from the Amplified Version and included in the reference line.

PART I

THE PROPHET'S PATHWAY TO MATURITY

CHAPTER 1

The Distinctives of a Prophet

There is no doubt that the call to the office of a prophet carries its own unique challenges. We see in scripture that all of those whom God called to this office had certain experiences in common while, at the same time, walking their own unique pathway. The particular combination of personality, upbringing, culture, and life experience that molds and makes the individual prophet is used by God to perfectly fit the needs of people, churches, and places that form part of the mandate given to that person.

The prophetic in general, and prophets in particular, have received much negative attention from the Body of Christ. Some of it has been well deserved, as unwise, immature people have acted foolishly. Some of it, however, has also been reflected over those who have not earned it, as is common in all areas of life—the innocent are accused with the guilty.

It is part of the enemy's plan to deny or discredit everything that God has called good, and imperfect humanity works in well with that plan. If denying and discrediting does not work, then deception is used as a major strategy to separate us from the plan of God.

I believe that the office of prophet and also that of apostle need to be established, recognized, and honored to help to bring this age to a close and enable the return of Jesus Christ to this world.

Apostles and prophets are called the foundation of the church, and I believe they bring strength and completion to God's plans when they work in harmony and unity with the other fivefold ministries.

The prophets see the picture, often with great clarity and, many times, far in advance of its timing but do not always know what to do about activating what they see. Apostles are trailblazers, people of drive and enthusiasm who know how to place structure around the visions and dreams of the seers.

In the following chapter, I will talk about the distinctives, which, when taken together, are indicators of a call to the office of prophet. There is quite a large time span between the call to an office and the commissioning to act in that office, and these distinctives will emerge over that period of time.

It is often only upon reflection that we can see a pattern that confirms or reveals such a call, but certainly, a true call will reveal itself as we are faithful to obey our God.

The emerging prophet often has the following:

1. A very early awareness of God and an exceptional hunger for spiritual things

The emerging prophet usually sees both demons and angels at a very early age and takes them for granted. All children are born with the ability to see the spirit realm, but emerging prophets are more sensitive to that realm and keep that faculty much longer than other children. They have a fascination for it, and if that is not directed to God and his word, such people will become involved with the demonic and New Age practices to satisfy their fascination.

2. Unusually challenging personal circumstances

An assignment of death and destruction seems to operate around that person's life from birth or before. Frequent sickness, violent and abusive family life, and near-death experiences abound in the life stories of emerging prophets. In nature, the time of birth is the time of greatest danger, and it seems that the demonic spirit realm can sense and identify a prophet at birth.

3. A very early sense of a call to ministry

God reveals their destiny to them personally and often in dramatic and unusual ways. Others can also see that they are different and recognize that call upon the emerging prophet, sometimes before they recognize or are willing to acknowledge it themselves.

4. A higher-than-average ability to hear God's voice

God is always present in their thinking, and a world without him cannot be imagined.

5. A strong desire to right injustice and deliver the oppressed and downtrodden

Prophets and apostles often become involved in politics and the establishment of charities as well as church outreach ministries.

6. When operating in the prophetic, a reputation for extreme accuracy

A tendency to "read the mail" is a foundational asset of the emerging prophet. Accuracy alone cannot be used to establish the credentials of a prophet. Even the demonic realm can be accurate although drawing that information from the wrong source. Extreme accuracy is, however, a baseline requirement as evidence of that prophet's mantle.

7. **A sense of weight and impact around the words they speak**

8. **A general sense of God's presence when they are speaking and even when they are simply physically present.**

From a very early age, in fact as far back as I can remember, I was always aware of God, always talked to him and expected him to talk back to me. I saw spirits of all sorts and had dramatic dreams. I had no idea then that everyone did not have these experiences, I just thought it was how life was. In the Bible, we see that Samuel was a young man who, from a very young age, was able to hear God's voice, although he needed to be trained to recognize this voice.

This training is a process that starts from birth and continues throughout our lives. Until a young prophet receives instruction from an experienced prophetic minister, or a mature minister who understands their process, they are likely to be confused and will be open to becoming involved in ungodly spiritual experiences like the occult or New Age.

The demonic realm attempts to seduce the prophetic child from an early age

I grew up in a home where poverty, violence, and alcohol abuse dominated my life. My parents were not Christians, but I was exposed to some Christian influence by a Godly grandmother, who read her Bible every day, and a very devout aunt and cousin.

It seemed like I was always hiding and trying to avoid my father, who was both angry and an alcoholic. Sometimes he lived with us and sometimes he did not, and I much preferred it when he didn't because of his unpredictable moods. His brother was just like him and was married to my devout aunt. I often witnessed her and my mother being the victim of physical violence and longed to intervene but was more inclined to hide.

This laid a wrong foundation in my life by creating a picture of an angry God to me. Although I automatically loved and sought God, I still had to let him heal these areas of wrong beliefs about him when I grew older. Absolute trust in God's goodness and integrity is essential for the emerging prophet to function at the high level that God requires of them. The enemy works hard to discredit God's integrity and loving nature in the life of the emerging prophet and also in the lives of all people.

Discrediting God's character places a barrier between mankind and God, which is very hard to overcome. This is why God focuses on developing faith and trust in our lives so that we can walk in dangerous places with him, knowing absolutely that he will bring us through. When we fail to grow in that faith and trust, we continue to depend upon our own ability to survive and grow. This limits our development and even gives a doorway to the enemy, which can cause us to live in a desert (Jeremiah 17:5-8). Trusting in the "arm of flesh," whether our own or somebody else's, instead of trusting God's arm to deliver us, keeps us in a wilderness of fear.

The highest level of the prophet's function can only be achieved through a close and unobstructed relationship with God the Father, Son, and Holy Spirit

At the age of eight, I walked into a church and announced to the startled nuns that I wanted to be a Catholic. They thought they had the next saint on their hands and proceeded to teach me everything about their faith and led me through the rites and ordinances of that church. At that time, this did not lead me to a personal connection with Jesus, although I know that many people in that church now walk with Jesus and know his power.

I did not know that it was unusual for a child of that age to so strongly choose a faith and inform their parents of their decision

This was evidence of a very early hunger for God and the boldness that would be needed to carry the mantle God was preparing for me. Holy boldness is essential in the life of a prophet, but sometimes through immaturity and lack of wisdom or training, that boldness looks like arrogance and causes that emerging prophet to be misunderstood and rejected.

Once again I did not consider myself to be different or unusual; it is only in retrospect that I realize how different I was and can make sense of the reasons why I felt I never fitted in anywhere. Often the feeling of being so different can make us feel unacceptable, when in fact, the difference is a defining factor of our calling. It is necessary to learn to identify differences created by our calling and differences created by a lack of direction and training from experienced prophets.

I spent three years enthusiastically embracing the Catholic faith, still without personally encountering Jesus, but God as usual had other plans and sent a lady who really knew Jesus to live next door to us. She had a beautiful singing voice, and I would often hear her singing worship to God; sometimes she sang in a strange language that I did not understand.

I was left alone for long hours, as my mother worked, and I started to spend a lot of time at this lady's house. She was warm and loving and accepted me as a part of her family.

She frequently spoke to me about my need to know Jesus. I was totally blind to this need as I had started to become blinded by religion and thought it was enough to take part in religious ceremonies. Although there are many people in all sorts of churches who know Jesus personally, at the time when I was in that particular church, I did not encounter any.

The enemy's plan was to distract me from real faith and relationship with God and bring me to a place of deception where I would think that religious ceremonies alone were starting to work.

Part of the enemy's plan is to cause us to be satisfied with the counterfeit, which is an imitation of what is real. The counterfeit always presents as truth; it is salted with truth and wrapped in truth, but its foundation is a lie. Deception is camouflaged so that we will find it appetizing.

One day, at the end of a forty-day fast that she had undertaken, my neighbor spoke to me again about Jesus, and for the first time I understood what she meant and, with many tears, met with Jesus. I was just eleven years old at the time.

Shortly after that, my family moved away from that area, and I was separated from the influence and strength of that lady. Her name was Marvena (Veenie) Hunter, and I will always honor her as my mother in Christ. The enemy likes to separate us from those who have great influence for good in our lives, but God will always surround us with such people. He is never short of prophetic relationships for us to connect with.

My father was enraged against me although I did not actually tell him about my salvation experience; he knew the difference between me following religious ceremonies and having a personal experience with Jesus. My mother was also converted, and one night after church, my father beat up the man who had driven us home. Another night we came home to find all our possessions thrown onto the front verandah and ourselves locked out of the house.

From the age of fourteen I moved into the home of a Christian family to escape his persecution. God rescued me in a miraculous way—I strongly suspect that my life was in danger from my father, who was totally irrational, full of rage, and had a serious drinking problem. About this time, I also found out that students in my high school planned to knock me off my push-bike with a car as I rode to school, and there was also an abduction attempt against my life. Each time God rescued me and hid me. Pharaoh could kill many babies but not Moses. When Jesus was born, God sent angels to warn his parents to leave and even told them where to go. God always has a plan and a way of escape. The enemy cannot kill us if we keep our hearts open to what God says. He will warn us in advance and show us the way of escape, which is often very unusual.

One of the distinctives of an emerging prophet is unusually challenging personal circumstances

I believe this is because the demonic spirit realm sees that prophet's mantle and tries to kill either the person or their ability to embrace their calling.

When an animal is born, predators circle to try and destroy that life at birth when it is most vulnerable, and this is a picture of the enemy's plan for all people, and especially the prophets who will bring God's voice to their generation.

Potentially, great resilience is formed in a person who must continually resist such attack. However, emotional wounding and brokenness is also a part of this process and must be healed so that resilience is not replaced by bitterness and a hardened heart.

King David knew that God requires a heart that is broken before him in a state or continual repentance for sin; that is a heart that God delights to live in and a person that God delights to flow through (Psalm 34:18).

We need to allow the Holy Spirit to so work in us that our wounded broken hearts are healed and supple and we stay in that place of sensitivity to him. The strength of the prophet is their sensitivity to God, but it is also their weakness, even their Achilles' heel. Sensitivity must be guarded, directed, and submitted to God. If it is not, then our souls, which are our emotions, mind, and will, become entangled with our spiritual discernment. This will create confusion and inaccuracy, a "mixture" that will defile our gifting.

God is able to take all of our circumstances, all of our pain and sorrow, and weave it into a picture of himself that will release and reveal who he is to ourselves and to others, if we allow him to. This will prevent us from becoming discouraged, angry people carrying bitterness and unforgiveness with our true potential bound up and even destroyed because of an inability to move on from past experiences. That which we offer to Jesus becomes purified and released again as sweet incense to others. The word "incense" means "to turn into fragrance by fire," and in the Old Testament, the incense was compounded to a special recipe given by God, which, when sprinkled on the hot coals of the altar, released a beautiful fragrance that covered the smell of the slaughtered animals.

Our flesh smells, but the incense of praise and worship will cover our cries as we die to ourselves. This is always a painful process, which if endured without a heart of faith and praise, and covered with words or thankfulness, just becomes offensive to everyone around us and unfruitful in our own lives.

In spite of, or perhaps because of, the persecution from my father, I was filled with the Holy Spirit and spoke in tongues during that year at the age of fourteen. This was a profound experience for me, just as my salvation was. It was truly real and changed my life. My boldness caused me to witness to everyone of Jesus, whether they wanted it or not! I also had a personal encounter with Jesus at the altar of a weekend Easter camp and knew that I was certainly called to serve him. I thought I needed to be a missionary, probably because back then, the only opportunities available to women were to marry a minister or go overseas as a missionary. I certainly knew, however, that God had separated me to himself.

I also preached my first sermon that year. I was asked to speak to the youth group, but when I arrived I found the church full and the street cluttered with cars. The whole church had turned out to hear me, as they had seen the touch of God upon my life. I had prepared for hours and had many notes but only remember that I spoke on the verse that said we should put on love, which was the bond of perfectness. All this in a year during which I had been kicked out of home for my faith, out of a church over a false accusation of gossiping, and had the lady who led me to Christ fall away in serious sin.

I was the only convert left that she had discipled. Somehow God kept me.

An emerging prophet has a very early sense of a call to ministry. God reveals their destiny to them personally. Others can also see that they are different.

God likes to explain the prophet's calling to them himself, and then he confirms it through others. God told me who I was; let God tell you who you are.

There is a tribe in Africa in which the father chooses the baby's name and tells no one until after the child is born and he has whispered it into the ear of the child. The child is the first one to hear his name straight from his father's mouth.

When the voice of authority speaks into our lives it imprints truth or error into our very DNA. When the voice of God speaks to us, it empowers us to do his will. God releases his authority and mandate from his spirit to our spirit; even in the womb we are called, we hear his voice. Other voices will intervene to try and separate us from the voice of our God. As we learn to separate the voices, we can follow the destiny God implanted in us in that place of development called the womb.

I married very young, and this marriage was, I believe, a strategic plan of the enemy to divert me from my destiny. The man involved had led a very ungodly life and, in spite of his conversion was never able to maintain Godly standards of purity. I was married to him for twenty-one years, and there was still no genuine repentance of that ungodliness. The marriage was concluded at that time.

When my marriage failed, I moved to a small country town, which I had not previously heard of, at God's direction. A lady I had accidently met, a genuine prophetic relationship, continually encouraged me to move to that town in spite of the fact that I was a city girl and did not at that time like the country. God confirmed this through several miracles of provision and an overwhelming sense of peace.

In spite of knowing I was in God's will, even after two years in that town, I was struggling to come to terms with a totally different lifestyle. I asked God "why does my life had to be so hard?", and he replied very clearly, audibly in fact, "It's because you are a prophet."

I can't find words to express how surprised I was. Prior to this I did not think I had any gifts. I had just started to prophesy in a limited way. I had no idea what a prophet should do and certainly thought they were Old Testament characters only.

After my salvation and infilling of the Holy Spirit, this was the third most defining moment in my life.

I sat on this information for three years, feeling that it was a secret between God and me and should be kept so. I was involved in the church in many areas, and the pastors saw potential in me that I did not see in myself. They trained me to teach a small group, counsel, preach, and help with church administration, all of which were a great foundation for the ministry God would lead me into as an itinerant prophet.

God always prepares people to connect with us divinely and catapult us into the next stage of his plan for us.

God did indeed have a plan for me, and I needed to be where he wanted me to be so that the plan could progress. He did not reveal my full destiny until I was positioned to start that journey.

Leaving and cleaving

Before each new season in our lives, God repositions us mentally, spiritually, and sometimes geographically.

The ability to be flexible and adapt to change is an essential factor in the growth and development of any Christian and especially that of a prophet. God is always working from his sovereign viewpoint and sends us on missions and assignments without revealing the whole picture to us. We may not see the whole picture until we are in heaven, when everything will be made clear. However, at present we see in part and know in part, and full knowledge and understanding will only come when we finally meet Jesus in heaven. We can know and must believe that God is always working for our good, to cause and even create good out of evil, our mistakes and failures, and out of the enemy's attacks against us.

If we are unable or unwilling to respond to God's directions without knowing everything, then our ability to complete his purposes is limited. It takes faith to obey God, and faith comes from our ability to be like Abraham and see the city afar off. Abraham followed the command of God to leave everyone he knew and go to a city that God had not even named to him. This was truly a faith walk and needed to be taken one step and one day at a time.

We need to see the city of faith that we are going to well before it is visible to our natural eyes. That city is the will and purpose of God for us, which he only reveals step by step, as our faith will allow us to sustain the vision. Without faith it is impossible to please God, and that sort of faith can only be in God's power and his ability to keep us and bring us to our promise and to his provision.

- God taught Adam about the one flesh principle, which causes and requires a man to leave his parents for his relationship with his wife (Genesis 2:24).
- God told Abraham to leave and cleave (Genesis 12:1).
- Jesus taught about leaving and cleaving to strengthen marriage (Matthew 19:2; 10:42).

Jesus also taught us that our desire and willingness to obey him must come before our desire to please anyone else. To leave means to forsake, and to cleave means to stick to like glue. Jesus tells us that if we love with *phileo* love, which means natural love of people for each other, our family, or anyone else more than we love him, then we don't deserve him.

He is not saying that we should not love them; indeed he commands us to love them. He is saying the love you have for me needs to be agape (God's special love, which comes from the throne room). That love takes precedence over brotherly love, and if there is a choice between demonstrating love for family, which would cause us to disobey God, then we must choose to demonstrate agape love toward God and obey him.

So the principle is to love family and to take responsibility for family members. If we have to choose between obeying God and pleasing family, however, then God requires us to obey him. I believe this does not mean to forsake responsibilities for young children or for marriage but to have a heart like Abraham, which would sacrifice his only son, the son through which the promise of God would have to come, to demonstrate not only obedience but faith and trust in God's greatness.

During season changes, leaving and cleaving is essential; we must forsake responsibilities that God would no longer have us involved in and stick like glue to responsibilities that he would have us take on. This also applies to relationships; discernment is needed during transitions times to recognize when God is sometimes changing the level of our relationship with some people. He is also adding new people into our lives for the new season.

In God's pressure cooker

I call my time in that country town my pressure-cooker time. God condensed a great deal of my personal growth into a very short time.

God can fast-forward your life and calling at any time. He is not limited to time, space, or circumstances. God calls you for your **kairos** *moment, the now time, and his times and seasons will be activated through your continuing obedience.*

Disobedience depositions you from the center of God's will. Your gifts will still operate, but you will seem to be marching in place, standing still, or even going backward.

Prophets are called and formed by God alone (Ephesians 4:11-12).

They cannot be made by the desire of man. The Bible tells us to desire spiritual gifts, especially prophecy, as these gifts bring comfort, edification, and encouragement; but the office of prophet and also apostle, pastor, teacher, and evangelist are specifically for the maturing of the church corporately and individually and the reproduction of lives and ministry gifts.

These offices carry governmental authority, and linked to that is a high degree of responsibility and accountability.

Authority and responsibility always go together; authority without responsibility and accountability is anarchy.

For some reason, some people strongly desire to be a prophet. Perhaps they see it as glamorous or powerful; however, if you try to walk in this office without having received it from God or if you try to walk in it before the time is right, you open yourself up to the same demonic attack as a prophet without the anointing and authority to combat it.

There is a continual need for a prophet to die to their own desires and reputation even as Jesus did so that they can be bold and not influenced by the criticism and misunderstanding that often follow the prophetic.

A prophet is a defender of God and his word and must always take the side of justice, truth, and integrity. He or she speaks for God and is very jealous and protective of their God's name and reputation.

Because of this, a prophet must overcome intimidation and the fear of man so that they are not influenced or controlled by people. We see this demonstrated when the commander of the Lord's army (an angel) was asked whose side he was on. He replied that he was here in God's name; he was on the side of what God wanted, not of party politics or the pleasure of man (Joshua 5:14).

The temptation to say what people want to hear will be constantly put before a prophet and must not be yielded to, as then we become an instrument of man and not of God.

A prophet is often different

The prophetic personality is unique. Each person has their own individual personality type and gift mix; however, those called to this office tend to have certain basic expressions of personality need that are essential to their functioning. The tendency of the mantle to shape a life is evident in certain aspects of personality both positive and negative. Every Christian must allow the continual working of the Holy Spirit to mold and shape them into the Christ likeness that they are born to be, including and especially his prophets.

High calling is no excuse for bad behavior; in fact God requires much more sanctification of those with high callings than he does of those who "stay by the stuff." Their personal value is equal, and their gifts also have equal value, but the consequences and effect on the lives of people is different; therefore, more is required.

God says, "To whom much is given, much is required" (Luke 12:48).

The words of a prophet even in casual conversation can have profound impact because of their gift and anointing. Even greater care is needed than what is asked of all Christians when speaking, as greater credibility is given to the words of a prophet from those who acknowledge the gift and greater power is released, whether intentionally or unintentionally, by the prophet.

Prophets crave solitude

The prophetic cave is not just for hiding from enemies and hearing from God; it is also a place to refresh the soul and process what God is saying and doing in their lives. The prophet frequently asks God why. They always like to know what God is up to in their lives and also the lives of those around them.

The prophetic mantle is very demanding, and people constantly draw upon it both intentionally and unintentionally. This creates an energy drain, which is physical, mental, and spiritual. Jesus perceived when virtue was drawn from him by the woman who touched his garment and withdrew himself from people for a season.

Prophets are very sensitive in both a negative and positive way

It seems that the higher the prophetic calling, the more sensitive a person is to spiritual atmospheres. Until we learn to recognize what we are responding to, we sometimes think it is a mental or emotional problem, when in fact our spirits respond to what is happening around us in the spirit realm.

In the Welsh mines, the miners used to carry canaries down the mine with them, as they knew that canaries had very sensitive lungs; and if there were any dangerous gases in the mine, then the canary would quickly die, allowing them time to escape before there was an explosion or before they lost consciousness because of foul air.

Prophets are like those canaries; they sense or feel or see dangerous spiritual atmospheres and need to learn to discern what God wants them to do about it.

Sometimes it is good to sound a warning so that everyone can leave the mine, and prophets and prophetic intercessors function as trumpets of warning and worship. Sometimes we have to leave the mine ourselves so that we do not die, because unlike the mine canaries, we are not locked in a cage; or rather if we feel caged, we should ask God for permission to leave. We may be in a place for a season, and when our mission is accomplished, God will move us on. We may not always see the results we want to see, but it is necessary to obey God and go when he says so, as we are sensitive enough that we can be easily damaged if we stay somewhere when God says to go.

During the journey of David from shepherd boy to king, there was a time when he became very confused by Saul's desire to murder him. He asked Jonathan, "But what have I done to Him to deserve this?" (1 Samuel 20:1)

David had yet to learn that some people could see and react to his mantle rather than to him as a person. They were not reacting to who he was in the natural but to what he carried in the spirit. Confusion is often created in the life of a prophet because of the reactions of people to their mantle. These reactions can include anger, jealousy, resentment, false accusations, and many other negative responses, which are basically an attempt to kill the carrier of the mantle so the mantle is destroyed.

A prophet has a higher-than-average ability to recognise God's voice.

Many times I heard God's voice but did not fully recognise it. This process of continually refining spiritual discernment enables the prophet to separate God's voice from the voice of many others.

Distinguishing factors about the voice of God

(Romans 8:16)

God's voice resonates in our spirit. His voice reverberates, vibrates, and resounds; it booms through our spirit. Our spirit says yes and agrees with God's voice. Sometimes, often in fact, our mind will challenge and disagree with what God is saying, but that inner witness of his spirit within us will produce peace in spite of our conflicting thoughts.

It is important to distinguish between soul peace and spirit peace. Soul peace is subject to circumstances and is very easily disturbed. Spirit peace, the peace that passes understanding that Jesus has left us, bypasses our natural thinking and is not affected by circumstances. The ultimate fruit of the voice of God is life, joy, and freedom, even though the things he says to us will also challenge and stretch us, removing us from our comfort zones to his purposes.

God's voice always points to Jesus, always points us to truth and does not create confusion. God's voice agrees with his word and witnesses to those mature spiritual authorities we have allowed into our lives. The word of God gives us the measuring standard, and in the mouth of two or three witnesses, every word of God will be established (Matthew 18:16).

A voice is intensely personal. In a room full of children a mother will always recognize the voice of her child, and we respond to the sound of our own name instinctively. A child in the womb learns to recognize the voice of her parents and responds to them by turning her head after she is born.

Modern technology has established that a voice is as individual as a fingerprint, and security systems have been set up to allow a person entry on the basis of their voice. The voice of God is programmed into our DNA, but before we come to know him, we have filters in the form of belief systems, frames of reference, and blind spots, which stop us from hearing him.

A frame of reference consists of those ideas and beliefs that we have formed through our society, family of origin, education, and peers. This is a framework through which we run all new information that comes our way. This can speak very loudly to us, and if we have not learned to remove this filter when we operate in the prophetic, it can color what we are able to hear from God, what we say, and how we say it. Sometimes God is able to get through to us in spite of this, and upon reflecting on my life I realize that although I often recognized the voice of God, there were also times when he was speaking and I was not hearing that voice, and times when I was hearing him but not understanding what he was really saying.

I did not then know that God would take me on a journey that would teach me to hear him even more clearly and to develop this skill through continual obedience to him in the finest detail.

Prophets tend to internalize everything they see and hear and don't always process it well.
Prophets usually feel and sense the poisons in the spiritual atmosphere before other people. They may be mentally confused or depressed without any known reason. Discernment needs to be developed so that it is possible to trace those vague feeling of unwellness, whether spiritual or mental, or even physical, to their source. Discernment is a spiritual gift, which is increased as we use it, and the growth of our discernment releases us to receive the strong meat of God's word and spirit (Hebrews 5:14).

To discern means to discriminate or distinguish, to separate the soul and the spirit, the demonic and the spirit of God (1 John 4:1-6).

Our spiritual ears need to be constantly tuned and retuned to God's voice because we are naturally inclined to interpret our world and the voices we hear through our five senses, and those senses constantly fight for dominance over our spirit. This can cause our spirits to be slightly out of tune if we don't remove the distracting voices from our environment.

Prophets are often very serious people.

They are so focused on the deep things of the spirit that they can become too intense and need to learn to find ways of connecting with people in a more lighthearted way. This can be very difficult, as often it is the very people around them who do not allow the prophet to function outside of the mantle and always expect a prophetic flow to come forth, often asking questions and requesting prophetic words every time they encounter that prophet. It can be very hard for a prophet to have a social life because of this.

Prophets speak words that are very accurate and carry a great spiritual weight. More and more their mantle is recognized by their peers, the people, and the demonic spirit realm.

As the prophet matures in their personality and spiritual perception, the mantle of authority automatically increases. When I was first being revealed as a prophet, after God had told me who I was, I found that people started to ask me if I was a prophet. I denied this, as I was not at all sure of myself. I was asked to minister prophetically at pastors' and leaders' gatherings, and it seemed like I always had the word of the Lord even when I was not aware of it.

I found I could just open my mouth when requested to prophesy, and a long stream of words, which were extremely accurate, would pour forth. God thrust me forward even though at the time I was fairly shy and certainly not seeking the limelight.

Suddenly I found my gift in demand and started to receive invitations to speak at churches and events. This happened without any effort on my part or attempt to attract these invitations. I was very surprised when it started to happen. God loves to surprise his servants and open doors for them that they have not sought. Truly our gift automatically makes way for us as we walk in obedience and love with our God.

The more I used the gift, the more it grew. God blessed me with favor and guided me wisely even when I did not know what the pitfalls of prophetic ministry were. God seemed to have blessed me with a certain naivety and innocence, and it was a number of years before I realized that I had to contend with people's attitudes about women in ministry and all the wrong expectations that people have about prophetic ministry, not to mention all the criticism that was out there about the prophetic because of those who had behaved unwisely with the gift.

If you are a prophet, there is no need to proclaim it; your gift will make way for you, and the fruit of your life will confirm it.

A prophet has a strong desire to change lives, churches, and societies. The prophet wars against injustice

This aspect of a prophet's call is often seen in the secular world. Some who are called to be involved heavily in these areas enter secular fields before they are Christians and some after they become Christians. Some get caught up defending animals and nature; some become movers and shakers in the business world. Misdirection of a call often happens although God does call some into the marketplace to minister. It is important to be the square peg in the square hole by determining what your current ministry field is.

I could never stand to see people hurt or unjustly accused. I always did and always do want to speak up for the underdog. When I hear that someone has been really blessed, my mind immediately goes to the person who did not get blessed. Sometimes I confused this and thought it was only about my own personal wholeness until I finally learned to separate the mantle from the humanity in my call.

A prophet is known by and should be judged by their fruit more than their gift. A gift is given and is not a reward for character or good behavior. Fruit is grown through the presence of the Holy Spirit within a life, continual obedience, death to self, and sacrificial service.

Fruit is the flavor the prophet leaves behind; what fruit remains after they go? Is it sweet or bitter? Are people blessed, changed, and connected to Jesus? These things determine the true integrity of a prophet

A prophet's words carry so much authority that great discipline is needed, even in everyday conversation, as the prophet's words have greater power to affect others even when there is no intention behind those words.

CHAPTER 2

The Prophet's Pain and Process

We see this process very clearly in the life of Jeremiah.

"Before I formed you in the womb I knew and approved of you [as my chosen instrument], and before you were born I separated and set you apart, consecrating you: [and] I appointed you as a prophet to the nations" (Jeremiah 1:5, Amp).

The word "formed" means "to squeeze into shape"; it is the same concept used when Jeremiah was told to go down to the potter's house and watch the forming and reshaping of the pot (Jeremiah 18).

God chooses a lump of clay (earth symbolic of man and water symbolic of the Holy Spirit) and forms and shapes it as many times and in as many ways as necessary, depending upon the state of the clay, its softness, and the shape it is to be.

The potter must keep the clay damp, bathed in the Holy Spirit so that it will form correctly; He shapes it with his own hands, he does not use an instrument, and then bakes and glazes it to just the correct strength to hold its shape.

God makes and remakes, breaks and rebreaks, builds and shapes the prophet again and again. In the end, the prophet will fling themselves upon the potter's wheel, longing to be made into a vessel that brings honor to God because they have come to a place where they only want what God wants for themselves and others. In this place of brokenness, the love and grace of God becomes truly real, usually because God has caused the prophet to see their own need for that love and grace by revealing the darkest, deepest parts of the prophet's life to them.

This revelation of who they are both with and without the love and grace of their God puts them in a position to extend that love and grace to others. Isaiah also went through this process when God called him to be his mouthpiece (Isaiah 6).

The vessel is formed for the use of the master, not for the comfort or pleasure of the vessel.

God also *sanctified or set Jeremiah apart*—made him clean and holy.

God then *ordained or appointed him* as a prophet to the nations.

Shaped, separated, and sent by the power of God, he is well-known as the weeping prophet, a man so sensitive to the heart and desire of his God he grieved on God's behalf because of the state of his people.

During a season in my life when I was in geographical transition, I pulled over during a long drive into an unusual road stop. It was originally a property developed by an immigrant family and was now both a road stop and a museum. The original chapel was still set up with a photographic record of the family's history. It had the original altar with a prayer book open upon it. It was open to Jeremiah 1, where Jeremiah receives his call from God. The chapter had been given a title: *"Don't forget who you are."*

This was an incredible shock to me at the time. I was taking time out for family reasons and had also started to wonder if, because of age, and some health issues, I needed to step back from ministry. God reminded me from a very unexpected source both who I was and who I needed to be.

God guards the work of his prophets carefully and jealously.

Jeremiah was called as a prophet from his mother's womb but did not receive his commissioning until his early teens or twenties. The exact age is not stated, but when he declared himself to be a child, the word used was one used to describe both infants and young men.

God's call usually comes to his prophets as a power encounter, a direct connection with God's voice and presence. Sometimes it starts as a slow awareness, at the very least, of being different from the people around them. A prophet needs a very clear mandate from God to operate in their office, as there will be so much challenge to it from both the spirit realm and people. Their minds will also create much confusion, as usually those who are called to this office start out as people who are not confident and do not desire recognition.

Sometimes this becomes corrupted in their lives as they develop confidence, and at this stage, God starts a process during which he strips them of all the fleshy manifestations that oppose the nature and character of Christ. All flesh inherits the tendency to desire power and glory. As I have mentioned before, the prophet becomes especially vulnerable to this because of the adulation of the people when they encounter the anointing and accuracy of the mantle the prophet operates under.

Jeremiah was called to his own people and to the nations; he was a prophet gifted with great power and authority to tear up and pull down national authorities both natural and demonic.

Jeremiah was told by God not to fear the people and their faces, and this was necessary as he continually faced death and destruction through his family, friends, and authorities (Jeremiah 11:18-23, 12:6, 20:1-2, 26:11, 37:15-16, 38:4-6).

This is a prophetic picture of the process all prophets will go through to one degree or another.

They may not face physical death, but they will surely face misunderstanding, criticism, and lack of recognition. As Jesus so clearly stated, a prophet has no recognition in his own country (John 4:44).

Lack of recognition and honor is not necessarily all negative; God will use it as a tool to refine the prophet's heart and is invaluable for training in humility.

We no longer physically stone prophets, but they are certainly stoned with words and rejection.

It is a lifelong lesson to learn to endure these seasons and yet keep your heart soft and pliable, free from anger, and especially bitterness.

Jeremiah's calling and commissioning were revealed to him in a short space of time, which is not always the case. We should consider the fact that the calling was there from the womb and before the womb. In the eternal plan of God, Jeremiah was foreordained to be God's spokesman, and then we can put some perspective on this.

We can realize that God was undoubtedly preparing Jeremiah in many unseen ways, which no doubt Jeremiah did not understand and was probably confused about, until God met with Jeremiah in what seems to have been a vision or dream and released the authority to act in his name.

The length of time between an awareness of the call and the release from God to walk in the fullness of that call can be quite far apart. We also need a release from those in authority over us. Otherwise, because we are not walking under delegated authority, we are outside of a place of spiritual safety.

God must purge the prophet of pride, presumption, self-pity, and inferiority.

Jeremiah, Moses, Gideon, and in fact all the prophets needed to be purged from the human weaknesses that most challenged them. We go from one extreme to another and will fall into the pits that our experiences and evaluations of life have opened before us.

Initially, Moses operated in presumption and anticipated his role by killing the Egyptian when God had not told him to do so (Exodus 2:12). He then moved into self-pity and false humility, not to mention a lot of fear, as he did not feel competent to go before Pharaoh. Perhaps he felt this way because he was raised in Pharaoh's house and knew they would look on him with familiarity, and they also knew his history of failure.

It is interesting to see that God sent Moses back to the very palace in which he had been raised; he was known to them as the abandoned Hebrew child whom they had rescued.

It is hard to lift your head and move on after public failure, and God often allows a prophet to make a major mistake or at least look like they made it, to keep them reliant on him alone.

Moses felt that inward call of destiny and, like all prophets, raged against injustice but did not necessarily know what to do with that anger and vented it in the wrong way and in the wrong time.

After forty years in the wilderness, he then needed to be released from the self-pity and inferiority that had surrounded his life because of his mistake. It seems that his temperament was now that of humility and meekness. The Bible describes him as the meekest man who ever lived; that, of course, is outside of Jesus himself (Ephesians 4:2, Numbers 12:3).

Meekness gives us a picture of humility, the ability to control emotions and not assert personal opinions, or demand our rights, except in the cause of justice.

When Moses went before Pharaoh, he needed Aaron as his spokesman because of his lack of confidence in speaking, especially, of course, speaking to the ruling heathen authority who would have had no hesitation in killing him. As part of the training process, God will take us to the old places of pain in our heart so that we can be healed and walk in authority over those things that previously intimidated us. Forty years before this, Moses had run in fear from Pharaoh; now he must go and face his fear. Perhaps he wondered if he would now be called to account for killing the Egyptian. God will not allow ghosts to haunt our lives; he must free us of those past ghosts so that we can walk in the authority that will set others free from the same ghosts.

Those people and places that are familiar to us can be used by the enemy to cause us to doubt the call of God. Jesus could not do miracles in his hometown because of their lack of faith; they just saw him as Jesus the carpenter's son, not as the Messiah.

Every prophet has to contend with the issue of familiarity.
Gideon immediately put his calling into the context of his family and his position in the family (Judges 6:15).

David was not even called before the prophet Samuel because he was the youngest and probably seen as the least likely to be the king (Judges 6).

Moses was also challenged by his family, Miriam and Aaron. The challenge was that he was no better than them. Again, familiarity is speaking. As the old saying goes, familiarity gives birth to contempt (Numbers 12:1).

Elijah could not do the same miracles in his hometown as he could when he left that area (1 Kings 17).

Jesus was not honored by many who knew him because they did not see the mantle of the Son of God, just the humanity of his known lineage and life experience (Mark :15).

The battle of the family must be fought and won, not with fleshly weapons but with weapons of the spirit. It is not necessary to try and convince family members, or even Christian family members, of your calling. Just react with love and grace and allow the Lord to heal your pain, and then release yourself from the expectation of receiving their acknowledgment and respect.

Leave all this in God's hands. He is the one who justifies and vindicates us. When we try to vindicate ourselves, we take this out of God's hands. 1 Corinthians 1:8 in the Amplified Bible gives us a clear picture of Jesus going into heaven's court to be our advocate and spokesman. He is the one who brings justice into our lives at the right time and in such a way that it cannot be refuted.

God defended Moses in both family challenge situations; God moved and showed his power on Moses's behalf. Allow him to do this for you too.

Godly honor given to God's prophets and other ministers opens up the blessing from that ministry.

Provision for the widow's current debt and future needs was created through obedience to the prophet; she obeyed the prophet, and by obeying Elijah, she demonstrated honor to his position.

Believing in the prophet means respecting the authority of their mantle, speaking of them with honor, and obeying the word they bring you, unless what they say disagrees with the word of God.

There were many lepers in Israel during Elijah's time, but none were cleansed except Namaan.

The prophet's reward

When you honor a prophet by acknowledging their mantle, you then receive what they bring to the table, the miraculous in any area, and the fullness of their mantle.

The degree of honor you give them determines the degree of the blessing you can receive from them. If you treat them as a good brother, then you will get the reward of a good brother only, which is limited to what the prophet can impart to you as a person.

If you honor a prophet as a prophet and receive the impartation of their gift, then you receive what they can impart from the supernatural realm.

If you are called to be a prophet, then you do not have to go through as much as they did in the development of their mantle (Matthew 10:41).

The Bible also tells us to "believe the prophets and live" (2 Chronicles 20:20).

The prophet Elijah came with the answers, but there was not enough honor given to the prophet in his region (2 Kings 5:9).

Nazareth also missed their miracles because of the lack of honor given to Jesus because of their familiarity with him. They knew him in the natural and only saw him in the natural, which caused them to be unable to access who he was in the spirit (Luke 4:27-24).

Nazareth was being given the "home ground advantage" but received Jesus only as a man so did not receive what he was offering them.

To honour means to respect the mantle, to believe what is said to them, subject to the judgement of the Word of God, to give to them financially, and to listen to and watch and read their teachings.

Pride and presumption

When pride and presumption start to be a less formidable giant, then self-pity often comes, especially when God does not respond how we would like him to.

Jonah is the classic example of this trait. It is very hard indeed to speak God's word and then see God react differently. Sometimes his grace is released, and where we expect to see judgment, we see mercy; our prophecies are misunderstood or misapplied and may appear to be wrong. This makes the prophet feel like they look really dumb. "What will people think?" they wonder, and this becomes a song that can play over and over in the mind.

Remember that God constantly deals with pride in the prophet's life, and either he will allow us to make mistakes or make it seem like we are wrong when we are not.

Prophecy is an art form and not a science—timing is involved, veiled speech and allegory is sometimes used, and the response of the person receiving the prophecy also affects the outcome.

Prophecies can be totally accurate but are always conditional upon the obedience and faith of the person receiving them. The prophet must continually contend with the expectation of the people with regard to their expected outcome of the prophecy. This includes the difference between what the people would like to hear and what God wants to say to them.

When God spoke to Jonah and told him to go to Nineveh, Jonah's response was to run as far as he could from God's assignment. This response may have been caused by fear and intimidation, inferiority, or perhaps some other reason we are not aware of.

His comment, however, gives us some insight into his reaction: "Is not this what I said when I was still in my country?" (Jonah 4:1, 2)

It seems that Jonah expected that the people would repent and he would look like he had made a mistake. No doubt the long journey and the spiritual pressure of carrying this message were included in his reaction. I believe he had a "why bother" reaction.

Discouragement can cause the prophet to feel that it is all too much trouble. People's expectations and attitudes and God's sometimes unexplainable responses make it all too much like hard work with little reward.

Elijah went so deeply into discouragement and self-pity that he was told by God to name his successor. *"And anoint Jehu son of Nimshi to be king over Israel, and anoint Elisha son of Shaphat of Abel-meholah* **to be prophet in your place"** (I Kings 19:16, Amp).

Supernatural discouragement is released by the Jezebel spirit when it is confronted by the prophet, and this discouragement can be so profound that the prophet will be de-positioned if he yields to it. It is very important to have an inner circle of friends who understand this and can help the prophet to fight against this force.

The prophet's pain comes through

- feeling God's pain caused by the unfaithfulness of the people he died for
- the rejection and misunderstanding by so many people of their calling
- the continual process, which God causes in their lives, to make and mold them and then keep them in the place of greatest fruitfulness
- the expectation and demands from people and pastors to constantly produce very accurate and effective words and directions.
- very long waiting times before they see the results of their sacrifice and prayers (Jeremiah 15:18)

Jesus is also described as a "man of sorrows and acquainted with grief." He is our great high priest, having overcome temptation and carried all our emotional, mental, and physical pain and sickness.

The prophet must live out their calling by personally overcoming what they will be anointed to release others from.

What we personally overcome becomes a rod of authority in our hands for others. Those who are especially anointed to release finance will often face huge financial challenges. Those called to minister emotional healing will face much emotional pain so that they can walk into their own healing and therefore release it to others.

It is the process of being made into the person who can walk in their ultimate destiny that produces the pain. Peter strongly declared that he would never deny Jesus; he appears to be full of pride, and it was necessary for that pride to be broken. It is only when we recognize our own insufficiency that God's power can truly be released in us.

Peter had to overcome his fear of man so that he could go on to be a bold and fearless spokesman for the gospel. He was called directly by Jesus, and he responded with faith, leaving his livelihood of fishing. Jesus told him to follow him and that he would make Peter a fisher of men (Matthew 4:18).

His greatest challenge came not when he left his livelihood but when he had to overcome great fear and acknowledge his connection with Jesus during the trial. He lost this battle, but Jesus later broke the power of the enemy in his life when he appeared at the beach after the resurrection and asked Peter three times to testify of his love for Jesus, not only with his word, which cancelled out his previous denials, but also by discipling the sheep who would follow Jesus after his ascension (John 21).

Although Peter did not totally understand that Jesus was asking him for agape (godly) love rather than *phileo* (brotherly) love, nevertheless, he expressed true repentance. We know his repentance was genuine by seeing the fruit of that repentance—a changed life that glorified Jesus and won many people to him.

Judas also denied Jesus but found no place of repentance; his heart had over a period of time become too hard to be softened. He cried tears of sorrow for the situation he found himself in; if they had been tears of repentance for what he had done to Jesus, he would have found repentance.

Peter went through the process that all prophets and fivefold ministers go through:

- Calling
- Testing
- Restoration and commissioning

God repeats this process as often as is necessary to realign the prophet with his purpose. We see this in the life of Abraham—on three separate occasions, at strategic seasons, God reminded him of his original promise. This also helps to refresh the word of God and shifts those discouraging voices that speak in both the natural and the spiritual.

The prophet's personal mantle is best grown in the house of God.

The corporate gathering of God's people has always been where God has placed his blessing. It is a part of the enemy's strategy to divide and conquer and separate God's people from the corporate gathering. The power of a gathering of Christians lies in the support, encouragement, and maturity that are produced by the connecting and interaction of the close fellowship of the local church.

Death is required to produce life, and we have to learn to die to ourselves through close relationships with others, which do not allow us to only please ourselves.

We see the dynamic of reproduction produced by death of the individual seed. If the corn of wheat falls into the ground and dies, much more corn will spring up from the death and breaking open of that seed. This is a picture of the life of the individual who is planted in a local church. The dying to self, which is produced by the close contact and interaction with a group of people who may think differently and have different personalities to us, requires a constant laying down of our own will. This is similar to but not as great as the marriage dynamic (John 12:24).

Becoming like Christ and being fitted into the local church in our gifting grows the church.

"Instead, we will hold to the truth in love, becoming more and more in every way like Christ, who is the head of his body, the church.[16] *Under his direction, the whole body is fitted together perfectly. As each part does its own special work, it helps the other parts grow so that the whole body is healthy and growing and full of love"* (Ephesians 4:15,16, Living Bible).

Being planted in the house of God allows us to flourish in the marketplace (Psalms 92, 2:13).

God's pattern for spiritual health has always been activated through relationship. God himself is a trinity, a small group. God longed for a family and so created mankind, and his words to Adam were that it was not good for man to be alone. Loneliness and isolation becomes very destructive to our emotional and spiritual health. We cannot grow in the things of the spirit unless we are positioned in relationship around people who produce a reaction in us that demands growth and change (1 Peter 2:5).

What we grow and mature in the house of God then becomes productive outside of the house of God. Maturity is produced in the house so that we can stand in the harsher environment of the marketplace.

Our calling needs to be transplanted at the right time by the Master Gardener.

He takes us out of a tight place so that we can grow and mature; the mature tree becomes a place of refuge to many. Our tendency is to want to remove ourselves from places of pain, but when we do this, we then have to go through the process that God is trying to put us through, at another time and place.

Our commissioning will occur in God's timing.

God alone knows when we are mature enough to be recognized and released as a prophet. When this occurs, we will carry the necessary anointing and favor to walk in the fullness of that calling.

From this process we will produce fruit that remains (Matthew 7:17-18; Jude, verse 12; John 15).

So God trains, corrects, and disciplines his children (Hebrews 12:5-13). Those who **submit** to his training will produce a harvest of righteousness. The *attitude* that we take to this process will determine whether circumstances make us grow stronger or weaker.

The tools that God uses to develop our character are the following:

1. The wilderness

Each time of new growth and anointing will be preceded by a wilderness. Jesus was baptized, and then anointed by the Holy Spirit with the voice of the father audibly declaring his love and his approval for his son. Then he was led by the spirit into the wilderness. It is easy to presume that hardship means that God is not pleased with us, when in fact it can be a sign that God is leading us forward into his perfect plan (Luke 4:1).

The wilderness that God leads us into is a place where we can only depend upon him even though we may not feel his presence during that season. It takes faith to maintain our walk with God and our ministry when we may be in a place of spiritual and emotional dryness.

The apostle Paul encountered Jesus on the road to Damascus in a dynamic way. He then went into the desert of Arabia for three years. I am sure that he needed this time to allow his thinking to change from a place of hating and killing Christians to a conversion experience, which would change everything about his life and turn his behavior around completely (Galatians 1:17).

Moses went voluntarily into the wilderness to escape retribution; whether God had preplanned this or merely allowed Moses to stay there until it was the right season for him to be revealed, we don't know. But when the time was right, God had to meet with Moses in a burning bush experience, to make him willing to move out of what had become a comfortable place for him (Exodus 2:15).

Sometimes people flee the call of God, and the wilderness becomes a safe place to them because it demands no change.

In the wilderness, the children of Israel had the same food and clothing every day, the same scenery and the same guidance, cloud and fire. This required no faith to adjust to changing situations. This type of faith, along with faith to believe God has not left us, is the faith that causes us to grow and mature.

John the Baptist, like many prophets, lived in the wilderness, partly as a place of separation from society and partly as a place where he could meet with God without distraction (Matthew 3:1).

In the wilderness
(Job 23:8-9)

- God seems to be hard to find.
- Personal prayer times can feel barren.
- It can feel like God is rejecting you, but he is just preparing you.
- You may appear to be going in the opposite direction to your vision.

God-ordained seasons of isolation, should cause us to press into God, refocus, and recharge. To get the most benefit from the wilderness, it is necessary to discern the seasons and to know whether we are in a wilderness because of our own sin and rebellion or because God has led us there to meet with us in a new way and to prepare us for new doorways of ministry.

2. Waiting

"*³For the vision is yet for an appointed time and it hastens to the end [fulfillment]; it will not deceive or disappoint. Though it tarry, wait [earnestly] for it, because it will surely come; it will not be behindhand on its appointed day*" (Habakkuk 2:3).

I like to call this God's waiting room. It is a time when everyone seems to get to the destination you want to get to or to the place they are heading for, before you.

These seasons must be endured with faith. The Bible says that it is only through steadfast patience and endurance that we will receive all of our promises (Hebrews 10:36).

Without faith in God's character, word, and promises to our lives, we will not maintain our momentum. During seasons of waiting to see our promises fulfilled, God is growing our capacity so that we will be ready to walk straight into the future when the door opens. Caleb waited forty years to receive his promise and finally went to Joshua and asked for his mountain. He said his strength was the same as when he was first given the promise. It is up to us to maintain our spiritual strength to be ready to conquer that mountain that we have waited for. God had not given Caleb some nice flat ground but a new mountain of challenge (Joshua 14:6-13).

God says that he will complete what he begins in us; faith and trust are needed in this promise to continue to see that city that cannot be seen with natural eyes. When the season is right, if we have maintained faith and spiritual strength, we will see and walk into our personal promised land. There will be giants, but we are well able to overcome them because we have maintained our mental, spiritual, and emotional strength during the time of waiting for the promise. If we don't do this, then our season of promise will come, and we will be unable to enter into it.

3. Temptation

The three areas that Jesus was tempted in were a representation of the temptation that faces all mankind. These are pride, greed, and lust for power or physical gratification.

> "*¹⁶For all that is in the world—the lust of the flesh [craving for sensual gratification] and the lust of the eyes [greedy longings of the mind] and the pride of life [assurance in one's own resources or in the stability of earthly things]—these do not come from the Father but are from the world [itself]*" (1 John 2:16, Amp, http://www.lockman.org/tlf/copyright.php#Amplified)

These three major areas of temptation are commonly called the girls, the gold, and the glory. We will constantly be tempted to sin in whatever area we are vulnerable to and probably some that we did not think we were vulnerable to as well. We need to always be prepared for the surprise attack, where we will be tempted to sin or disobey God in areas of our lives that we thought we were strong in. A life of submission to God's will and a laying down of our own will as demonstrated by Jesus will keep us protected, and the Holy Spirit will also speak to us and warn us if we allow him to.

David prayed that God would keep a watch before the door of his mouth to help him guard his words, and I believe we should also regularly ask the Holy Spirit to warn us of the enemies' snares. An invaluable protection is also to have a hedge of spiritually mature friends and intercessors in our lives, to whom we have given permission to speak to us about our weaknesses and also any problems they see developing in our lives.

James speaks about temptation, saying that God gives us grace if we humble ourselves so that we can resist the devil and submit to God. Overcoming temptation is always a twofold process, to stand firm against the thoughts and opportunities the enemy places before us and to humble ourselves under God's hand of correction and guidance, acknowledging our need of his strength to help us in the battle.

Lucifer fell from his place of heavenly authority because of pride, self-will, and rebellion; he exalted his will, but Jesus submitted his will to the Father by living in the opposite spirit and therefore purchased back the power to walk an overcoming life for himself and for us.

Part of the end-time assignment of the enemy against all ministers of God's word and especially the prophets is to cause them to fall into sin, which will destroy their ministry.

We have seen many good men and women of God fall into sin, especially in the last twenty years, and we all need to be on our guard against this.

We will constantly be tempted to sin in actions, words, and attitudes.

4. Criticism and Offense (Matthew 18:7)

One of the main areas that we need to guard against is that of offense. Offense means a scandal or a stumbling block and is a major reason why many Christians are out of fellowship and out of ministry. Jesus said that offense would cause many to fall away from him (Matthew 24:10).

"Offense" means: 4625, skandalon, skan-dal-on (scandal); prob. From a der. Of G2578; a trap-stick (bent sapling) i.e. snare (fig. Cause of displeasure or sin):—Occasion to fall (of stumbling), offence, thing that offends, stumbling block.

False accusation, criticism and offense will always come against us, (2 Corinthians 6:8-10)
But as Jesus did not defend Himself, so we should also (Acts 8:32)
let Him, He will be our vindication (1 Corinthians 1:8)
(Psalms 57:3)

We can choose to take offense or to let the offense go. Those who love God's word will not take offense. (Psalms 119:165)

Key areas of offense come

- against spiritual leaders when our gift is not acknowledged.
- against other Christians when they are promoted above us. (Hebrews 13:17)
- against God when we feel he has let us down

Chapter 3

The Prophet's Personal War

The word of God and the development of those who proclaim it will always be challenged by the enemy. Unfortunately much of that challenge comes directly through people. It is important to discern when a spirit is manifesting through the words and actions of others. If we separate the person from the spirit, in our thinking, it is easier to respond in a godly way to the person while also using spiritual weapons to bind the operation of opposing spirits.

The following spirits commonly manifest against the prophet:

1. **Jealousy—God uncovers and reveals his hidden prophets, and the uncovering activates jealousy, false accusation, and persecution.**

When my prophetic mantle first started to operate publicly, the first thing I noticed was that certain people seemed to hate me without a cause, or at least without a cause that I could see and understand. In my thinking, I was just myself; it was not until I learned to recognize that when others looked at me they often saw the mantle and reacted to that, so they became very angry with me or frightened of me.

This is not always the case, but the prophetic anointing certainly activates issues and demonic forces in people's lives. At other times, it seems that God "hides" the prophet again and people see only their humanity. This can also activate jealousy or the "older-brother syndrome." Jesus saw this again and again as he ministered on earth. To many, he was just Jesus the carpenter's son; they saw only his humanity and genealogy. To the Jews genealogy was very important, even excessively so. I believe this is because the Messiah's genealogy was prophesied in scripture, and so they looked to the natural without understanding the divine miracle of supernatural conception.

People can become confused, angry, and jealous against the prophet because they do not understand why God will use that person more than others. They have not seen the divine genealogy, that divine seed which births and activates the prophet's mantle at the appointed time as the prophet walks in sanctified humanity and divine anointing. Many people do not understand the process that the prophet goes through in the unseen places until eventually God allows their gift to be seen.

Jealousy manifests in words, which are essentially death wishes spoken over the ministry and in actions designed to discredit

The classic example in the word of God is that of David and Saul.

To successfully process this experience, it is necessary to learn to separate your mantle from your humanity. David was confused about why Saul would want to kill him. He did not yet understand the power of his mantle or how it would affect others.

"Then David fled from Naioth in Ramah and went and said to Jonathan, 'What have I done? What is my iniquity and what is my sin before your father that he seeks my life?'" (1 Samuel 20:1)

In David's own eyes he had done no wrong; in fact he had done only good toward Saul, but his mantle caused a spirit of jealousy and murder to arise against him. It is part of the price the prophet pays, which challenges the flesh nature of those around them. People then need to make a choice about their response, but the prophet cannot allow their attitude to that person to become judgmental in a fleshly way. If this happens, then the prophet will start to receive seeds of that criticism and judgment in their hearts that will pollute their gift.

Avoiding this attitude teaches us to deal with personal injustice in a way that causes us to walk victorious over the spears and arrows of the enemy.

Jealousy was birthed in the world when Cain killed his brother, Abel, and is commonly seen in children and adults. It will especially target those whom God is using to speak his word, and it likes to silence the genuine prophetic voice so it can speak the words of deception and take the glory for itself.

Jealousy speaks and says, "It's not fair. You have what I want, and you don't deserve it, but I do."

It is an immature reaction against what is perceived as injustice. It is impossible to judge these situations without all the knowledge about the other person's life, and only God has all that knowledge. It is important to keep our hearts clear of criticism; an attitude of criticism will produce ungodly judgments against others. This will then cause us to reap those judgments.

2. False Accusation and Loss of reputation (Matthew 18:7)

One of the hardest seasons to walk through is that season when we are falsely accused as we are facing a situation that we are usually powerless to fix. There is a time to keep our mouths closed and a time to give a wise answer to an accusation. For instance, Jesus did not open his mouth as he went to the cross, but when he was accused of being Beelzebub, he gave a wise answer to his accusers. False accusation is an integral part of the Christian life, as is criticism. It is easy to take offense and want to retaliate; however, there is a pathway of greater maturity, which is one that allows Jesus to be our vindicator.

"And He will establish you to the end [keep you steadfast, give you strength, and guarantee your vindication; he will be your warrant against all accusation or indictment so that you will be] guiltless and irreproachable in the day of our Lord Jesus Christ [the Messiah]" (1 Corinthians 1:8, Amp, http://www.lockman.org/tlf/copyright.php#Amplified).

We will often be accused of what we would not do, rather than what we would do. The weaknesses of our flesh nature usually have a consistent pattern in each individual, and we become aware of the areas we are likely to fail in, and so do others.

When we are accused of something we would never do, then our indignation arises and can create a blind spot, as we think that we would never do that; therefore, how dare people accuse us of that.

It is a manifestation of our self-righteousness, the Pharisee spirit that then creates an ungodly response that can grieve the spirit of God as much as if we did fall into that particular sin.

The enemy sees many of our weaknesses, people see some of our weaknesses, and we see some of them. Some are hidden from us in blind spots, which only the Holy Spirit can reveal, as he sees all of them and will reveal them to us if we are open to receiving this revelation and changing accordingly.

As we mature we learn to guard our weak areas, but often, perhaps because of pride, we don't guard what we see as our strengths. In times of war, defense forces evaluate the strengths and weaknesses of what they are defending and of their troops and provisions and deploy their resources accordingly.

When an enemy launches a surprise attack, they will launch it against the area where it is least expected, or least defended.

False accusations wound our pride and our flesh, and we can then rise up in self-righteousness, declaring we would never do that thing. The power of false accusation lies in this very reaction. It attempts to smear our character and reputation. Above all things we value our reputation—that is, what people think of us. God desires to get to the very root of pride in our lives and will allow us to be slandered, misunderstood, and falsely accused.

In the garden, the enemy's first tactic was to smear the character of God, telling Adam and Eve that God was trying to keep their heritage from them. God desired and had created them in his image; he wanted them to be like him and wanted to release an understanding of his ways and nature to them. Satan was falsely accusing God himself (Genesis 3).

Jesus was called Beelzebub (dung god); there could be no worse accusation than that. He was accused of casting out demons through the power of the demonic, an accusation that did not even make sense (Matthew 12:26).

The enemy loves to cast lies about character, motivation, and the source of the prophet's power so that he will divert attention from what God is saying through the prophet. If he cannot seduce the emerging prophet into polluted power sources and sin, which defiles character and the gift of God, he will accuse the prophet of the very areas of sin that he would have liked to draw him into (Matthew 10:24, 25).

3. Jezebelic Onslaught

Jezebel always forms an alliance with people who are in places of authority; it is especially attracted to those who will, for whatever reason, **allow** it to operate against those who carry God's power and **enhance its ability** to operate against those who carry God's power. When it confronts the prophet, it operates through people who are in alliance with those in places of authority within the church. Those who carry governmental authority in the local church have, either by explicit permission or by omitting to bring boundaries and discipline to the person manifesting Jezebelic power, allowed the operation of this spirit.

When this spirit operates because it is in alliance with someone who enhances its operation, it is particularly powerful. We see this in 1 Kings 16:30-33. Ahab is described as "doing more evil than all the kings before him and also more to make God angry than any other King," not to mention raising up the altar of Baal and leading the way for his people to engage in child sacrifice. He is attracted to Jezebel and she also to him, and together they increase their power to try and wipe out all the prophets in Israel, especially Elijah who was the chief prophet at that time.

I believe we will see more and more of this alliance of Jezebel and people in authority manifesting in the end times, even within the church, which has not allowed the purging of the Holy Spirit in its midst.

There are various levels of manifestation of Jezebelic power through individuals, and they are determined by that individual's vulnerability to it and also the amount of permission they are given by church authorities to operate through position in the church and through undisciplined behavior in the church.

Mature Jezebelic power is not seen often and I believe only operates through people who have fully given themselves over to this spirit. People who manifest some aspects of Jezebelic power are not and should not be called Jezebel.

Much has been written about Jezebel, and I will not attempt to fully expound the effects of this spirit; however, I would like to summarize the ways in which it launches against the prophet and indeed all who will follow Jesus and speak his word.

Jezebel's goal is to slaughter, massacre, and cut down God's prophets and those churches that walk in God's power. It aims to take their strength, their reputation, and their ministry mantle from them (1 Kings 18:4).

All Christians can hear God's voice and speak his word to one degree or another, but the prophet carries a depth and degree of the word of the Lord that is greater and more powerful than those who don't wear the prophet's mantle. The prophet carries a degree of spiritual authority that can directly address high-level demonic spirits and has the power to bind them to a greater degree than those who do not carry that mantle.

4. False accusation empowered by demonic forces

This is much stronger than the previous false accusation I spoke about; when it is empowered by Jezebel it pierces the soul. It is like the knife in the heart feeling that causes and opens the door to supernatural discouragement. Elijah was accused of troubling Israel. He was strong at this stage and able to refute the accusation. I believe, however, that this was the start of the assault against him and that somewhere, that accusation stuck to his soul and became an opening for the later assault of profound discouragement (1 Kings 17-22).

We are always accused by Jezebel of the opposite of what our intentions are. In the process of the prophetic operation, there is disturbance of the atmosphere and even a troubling of the atmosphere and situations of the people, but this is God's shaking that he instigates and allows (Hebrews 12:27).

God shakes or troubles for the purpose of blessing; the enemy shakes or troubles for the purpose of destruction.

The innocent will always feel guilty under the accusation of Jezebel. There is a twisting of words and intentions, which is specific to Jezebelic attack, and this can infiltrate the mind and soul of the person under attack.

The mantle is often destroyed or laid aside through massive intimidation, supernatural discouragement, and false accusation.

5. **Enthronement of false prophets for the purpose of depositioning the true prophets (1 Kings 18:26-29)**

Let us look at this pattern in the life of Elijah

We see that the prophets of Baal first *counterfeited the Levitical law*. They offered sacrifice and called upon their demon gods to endorse the sacrifice with supernatural fire. The demon gods could not do this because they were bound by the presence of the true prophet Elijah; his words of scorn disempowered the demon gods.

Baal's prophets then proceeded to use *their flesh* to activate their power by cutting themselves as a picture of human sacrifice. We see this manifested today as troubled people say they find release from their pain through cutting their flesh. (I believe this is transference of that original spirit, which seeks broken people to activate through. When their emotional pain is healed by Jesus, then that spirit of cutting can no longer manifest in their lives.)

The false prophets then *counterfeited spiritual gifts* by false prophesy to try and activate the power of their gods.

This is the pattern the enemy consistently uses to enthrone himself where possible.

They failed to deposition Elijah initially because he still operated in faith and did not allow that faith to be overcome by the force of the enemy, which was ranged against him.

6. Supernatural discouragement that produces loss of strength and endurance

After that amazing miracle, or series of miracles, as miraculous fire consumed water-soaked rocks and wood and dust, the full power of the demonic was launched against Elijah. Ahab then told Jezebel what had happened, or at least his version of what had happened. He did not speak about the attack of Baal's prophets against Elijah but just stirred up Jezebel's hatred of prophets using a part truth.

The enemy uses part truths to accuse and discourage, with an emphasis on the lie, but just enough truth in the accusation to give the impression of total truth.

Under the extreme oppression of this spirit, which was launched by Jezebel's words of death over Elijah's life, Elijah faced the choice to confront it or to run from it. He was probably very tired after his last power encounter; no doubt his body craved rest, and his spirit and his soul were also exhausted. In that place of vulnerability, under the enemy attack, he started to make mistakes.

- He isolated himself. He left his servant at Beersheba, the place of the well (1 Kings 19:1-21).
- He left the place of the well, where there would have been spiritual provision.

- He deliberately went into the wilderness and confessed death.
- He believed the lie "I am not better than my fathers."
- He ate the angels' food but lay down again.
- He lost his perspective and only remembered what the enemy had done—"they have torn down your altars." He forgot that he had rebuilt the altar of the Lord.
- He believed in his aloneness.

Twice God asked him what he was doing in that place, the place of lies and discouragement and aloneness; and twice Elijah replied with a description of what the enemy had done instead of an acknowledgment of God's power in that situation.

7. Submitting passively to the attack of Jezebel

Elijah was depositioned by his response to what Jezebel had done, and from that point, his mantle began to be transferred to Elisha (1 Kings 19: 16-19).

The prophet needs an inner circle of friends who understand the prophetic process and can discern when they are under Jezebelic attack and warn them. When the deep discouragement starts, it becomes very difficult for the person under the discouragement to see what is affecting them. They will interpret what they are experiencing and feeling as real and internal, when in fact it is all exterior and launched upon them by the demonic spirit realm.

In the garden of Gethsemane, Jesus sweated great drops of blood under the mental and physical and spiritual pressure he was experiencing. He was undoubtedly surrounded not only by angels but also by the forces of hell itself that had come to watch the Son of God suffer.

Jesus demonstrated the response we all must have to overcome the assault of the enemy against us. He aligned himself with the will of God. The will of God is found in the word of God, and as the word is truth, truth always clears away deception. God eventually told Elijah that he had reserved seven thousand who had not bowed the knee to Baal.

Elijah could not see that truth for himself because he had aligned himself with the lie of the enemy by only remembering and declaring what the enemy had done and not what he had done through the power of God.

8. Fear and Intimidation (Jeremiah 1:8)

When God called Jeremiah He specifically told him that he must not fear the faces of the people to which he was sent.

Fear and intimidation continually stand before the prophets to cause them to back off and turn around from their mission.

At every stage and level of authority these two giants must be warned against. David famously demonstrated this war when he encountered Goliath.

Fear speaks about the size of the giant—intimidation speaks to our identity.

Fear says the giant is too large—intimidation says that we are too small to overcome that giant (1 Samuel 17:11).

Goliath was standing on a mountain fully armed. He called out loudly, speaking a challenge to the army of Israel. Intimidation always speaks loudly, shouting in our ears the words intended to close our ministry down. Israel became "dismayed and greatly afraid" when they heard the words and saw the size of the giant. Their natural senses told them that this was a large problem indeed, as they apparently did not have a man who could go against Goliath. They allowed the giant to set the parameters of the battle.

David had been prepared by God in the wilderness, killing a lion and a bear and learning to depend upon his God to help him overcome these beasts. He was sent by his father on what was a natural mission to take food to his brothers, but in fact this was a God assignment, which would launch him into the next level of his destiny, if he allowed it to.

David heard the challenge of the enemy, and he was the only person who heard it who was not full of fear and intimidation because of that challenge.

David recognized two important facts about this battle:

- **People in covenant with God have giant killing power.**
- **People who recognize and draw upon that power can kill any giant.**

The giant was coming against the nation of Israel, and he was uncircumcised. Circumcision is a sign of covenant with God, and Goliath was trying to destroy the nation that was birthed through covenant with God and sealed by the act of circumcision. Because he was not in covenant with God and Israel was, he could not defeat them. He could only speak such fear and intimidation over them that they would run away from him and defeat themselves.

As David started to declare the weakness of the giant, the assault of false accusation rose against him through his brother. He was accused of having a proud and insolent heart and also of deliberately coming to see the battle. Neither of these accusations was true.

David kept his focus on the big picture, declaring, "Is there not a cause?" (verse 29) and not answering the false accusation.

False accusation will take our attention if we let it, and we will lose sight of the battle and the assignment of our God.

David also faced the intimidation that came against him through Saul. Saul simply stated the truth as he saw it, telling David he was too young and inexperienced to go against the giant.

David described his experiences with the lion and the bear but also spoke in faith out of his revelation of God's strength in his life. He said, "The Lord who delivered me . . ." (verse 36).

David used the weapons he was trained in, his slingshot, but prophetically declared to the giant that he came in the name of the Lord

This prophetic declaration destroyed the spiritual power behind the giant and killed him more surely than the stone that hit his forehead.

David was then able to cut off his head with the giant's own sword.

The Lord will release us to destroy that which comes against us with the very weapons intended to kill us, if we don't allow fear and intimidation to speak to us.

The words of David, which were full of faith, overcame the words of Goliath, which were full of fear and intimidation.

CHAPTER 4

The Prophet's Impact and Influence

Prophets make an impact both by their words and by their presence. They are one who influences atmospheres, people, cities, and nations. The breath of God is released by the prophet's words.

Prophets have the following:

1. Power to create

God spoke, and the Holy Spirit moved upon the waters. Those anointed words released God's power. God has delegated the authority of life-changing words to all Christians and also given extra governmental authority to prophets and other fivefold ministers.

For this reason a prophet, and also the other fivefold ministers, must be very wise and careful, even in ordinary everyday conversations.

Jokes and lighthearted words can and do have extra power when spoken by anointed ministers and will therefore have a far greater effect than the words of others who do not have this gifting.

Much authority is given to prophets, and much responsibility must be exercised by those prophets to whom it is given.

When Ezekiel spoke to the valley of dry bones, they came together; each bone in its appointed place, he spoke again, and skin and sinews were miraculously created and attached themselves to the skeleton in exactly the right place. He spoke again and the breath of life came into them and they formed a great army (Ezekiel 37:1-7).

A prophet causes the coming together of plans, purposes, and destinies in individual lives and churches. He or she releases life and direction into areas of stagnation or death. The prophet can create and sustain momentum.

2. Power to clear the way for God's will

Isaiah prophesied about the coming of John the Baptist, who was sent by God to prophetically declare and clear a way for the Son of God to be received. He declared a clearing away of the obstacles so that change could come and God's will be accomplished (Isaiah 40:3-5).

The voice of the prophet brings change and release and activates destiny in the lives of those to whom it is addressed. God's word does not return empty but will fulfill God's purposes (Isaiah 55:1).

3. Power to release healing

Jesus declared his mandate to be a releasing of the captive in all areas—physical, mental, emotional, and spiritual—for the purpose of a rebuilding of the lives of the people (Luke 4:18, Isaiah 61).

Healing is an integral part of the prophet's mantle, although some will manifest it in different ways to others.

Without healing and restoration, destiny cannot be accomplished. People are limited by their emotional wholeness, and sometimes when a person cannot make forward progress no matter what they do, it is because they need a new level of healing and restoration.

4. Power to reproduce

A vital function of fivefold ministers is reproduction of ministry gifts in the people and the church and the training and maturing of the Body of Christ. This takes a certain level of maturity on the part of that minister, as our flesh always seeks personal glory; and the temptation to hold gifting to ourselves so that we may get the glory will always rear its head.

We can only successfully reproduce what we have allowed to mature in our own lives. If we reproduce our weaknesses then the spiritual children we give birth to will reflect more of our weakness than our strength.

The prophet has a responsibility to allow the work of the Holy Spirit to bring them more and more to that place of maturity so they can fulfill their mandate to bring others to maturity.

Prophetic schools are often started by prophets, and only a prophet can train another prophet.

I had never even attended a prophetic school, and yet in the first year after I moved to the large church where I was on the pastoral staff for many years, I was asked to form a prophetic school.

My spirit leaped initially, as it does when our primary passion is touched, and I quickly drew up a list of subjects and started a school that ran for four days. The first school had only eight students, and as I discussed it with my senior pastors, consideration was given to cancelling it.

My enthusiasm prevailed, however, and it has now run continuously for ten years, often having more than one hundred students at a time from many different church streams. I have also taken it to France, England, and the United States, not to mention Poland and other European nations.

I love to see the impact and changed lives of the people who do the school; many have done it more than once, and the curriculum has changed and evolved with time.

Mantles are for reproducing and passing on to others, not for hoarding in dark cupboards.

5. Power to activate the presence of God

When a prophet or a company of prophets was present in the Old Testament, the overflow of prophetic anointing activates people around them to prophesy. Those who had never prophesied and probably never would again spoke the word of the Lord. Saul was anointed by Samuel and commissioned to be a prophet among the other prophets.

They had been schooled in the prophetic and Saul had not, yet God anointed him to a greater degree than the schooled prophets. God gave him a different heart. Some of the schooled prophets despised him as is always the case when God raises up someone whose true destiny has been hidden.

Saul hid himself among the baggage; at this stage he had a humble heart and did not seek promotion. Most prophets have been dragged kicking and screaming into their role. If they can maintain a humble heart, then God can continue to anoint them. If they walk away into pride, misuse of power, and a desire to take God's glory, then sooner or later they will fall (1 Samuel 10:10, 19:21).

Moses also spoke the word of the Lord to the people, and after he had gathered the elders, the Lord himself came down in a cloud and took of Moses's anointing and placed it upon the elders so that they also prophesied. Two men remained in the camp and prophesied among the people, and when Joshua complained that they had not moved to the tent as the others had, Moses declared that he would like to see all God's people prophesy. After this, the Lord fed the people with fresh quails but also judged those who had walked away from his statutes with plague (Numbers 11:24-29).

An extra release of the prophetic anointing uncovers and judges sin because sin cannot stay in God's presence.

Prophecy, especially when it is spontaneous and corporate, is a manifestation of God's increased presence. Jesus is always with us, as the word says he never leaves us or forsakes us, but the outward presence of God, which envelops us and activates revelation and miracles, is released either as a divine act or through the presence of those who carry that mantle of his glory.

In the book of Acts, God descended in power upon the disciples as they waited in obedience; this produced supernatural tongues, prophesy, power, and miracles in the lives of those touched by it.

Those called to the office of prophet are never neutral and never satisfied with the status quo. They have opinions and need to learn to separate their own opinions from God's desires.

Great wisdom is needed in the expression of the word of the Lord and learning how and when to share that word. I will say more on that later.

Because a high-level of revelation is a strong feature, indeed a distinctive of the prophet, the balance of revelation and action takes time to get right. Moses initially knew his destiny and mission quite clearly. He had the prophet's desire for justice; he did not, however, have an understanding of God's timing and godly processes when activating destiny.

He anticipated his mission to set his people free by allowing anger to control his actions. Much later, more than forty years in fact, this very anger was to deposition him so that he was only allowed to see the promised land and not to enter it.

Faith is needed in the operation of the prophetic, not presumption that we are infallible, but faith in God's willingness to speak through us as we live a yielded and obedient life to him. Faith also should determine our ability to reach into the depth of our gift and speak those things that truly seem strange to our natural minds.

I have found that the less sense a prophetic word makes to my natural mind, the more likely it is to be very accurate. It takes faith to stay in that realm of the spirit, speaking the word of the Lord, but also faith to know when the flow has stopped and to cease speaking when God ceases anointing those words. The natural mind will say continue and keep speaking because that makes no sense to my mind. It seems to need an explanation. Those who operate in faith will be led by the still small voice of God, and he knows when enough has been said.

One of the key elements of the prophetic is the ability to discern when we have stepped out of the flow of the Holy Spirit and into our natural mind.

Faith connects us to that flow and lets us know when it has stopped because faith is the ability to see with the eyes of our spirits and not with our five senses.

Jesus said that his words are spirit and life, and all prophetic words should ultimately bring life (John 14:10).

A recognized prophet is released

- to bring direction (Acts 11:27-28).
- to bring correction (1 Samuel 2:27).

- to ordain and activate ministry gifts (Acts 13:1-3, 1 Samuel 16:13).

When a recognized prophet is ministering, these functions will automatically operate; when a person is operating in the gift of prophecy, none of these functions should be seen.

God himself determines the authority boundaries, and when we operate outside of God's boundaries, we open ourselves up to demonic attack. The enemy recognizes God's boundaries although he does not like to obey them himself, but he knows when we are outside of the area that God has authorized us to operate in.

Both men and women are called and ordained by God to walk in fivefold ministry gifts. The book of Joel clearly teaches that the outpouring of the spirit is upon men and women and children. The first part of this prophecy was fulfilled in Acts 2, as the former rain.

The latter rain is yet to fall, although there have been many instances of outpourings of various lengths. There will be a final outpouring of power to quicken God's victorious end-time army and release signs, wonders, and miracles, which cannot be disputed and will restore the balance of power back to the Body of Christ and away from the enemy (Revelation 11:6).

Judgment will also be contained in that end-time outpouring; once again we saw some of that in the judgment of Ananias and Sapphira in the early church, and it was just a foretaste of what will be involved when God truly pours out his spirit.

We need to know that when we ask for revival, we will receive some things we were not asking for. Judgment must begin at the house of God; he is auditing his church, and those who allow this auditing will be able to receive the blessings of revival without the judgment.

One of the roles of the prophets that God is raising up will be to activate outpouring in various places. Sometimes their very presence will do that, sometimes their words will be released to do that, and always God will direct them sovereignly.

The new generation of prophets will be like no other before it; they will carry the authority and the mantle to wind up God's final plans for his creation before he returns to claim back his possessions. These prophets are mostly hidden at present. Certainly their full potential is hidden.

Jesus told a parable about the wheat and the tares growing together until the harvest; and God will send in the harvester to separate the false, counterfeit, and rebellious self-proclaimed prophets or those who are indeed called but not walking in obedience from those who are truly called, have submitted to God's processing, and are ready to lay down their lives for his purposes.

CHAPTER 5

Separating Truth and Error

The enemy counterfeits every aspect of the gifts and mantles God has given to his church.

Aspects of the counterfeit:

- The counterfeit draws attention to an individual
- The counterfeit takes attention from the leader
- The counterfeit overrides our free will

There are many voices that try to take our attention, all varieties of demon, our mind and emotions, our society through media, our friends and even our enemies. Although the ability to hear God's voice is in our very DNA and he is always speaking, our radar is jammed by those many voices.

It is necessary to identify and eliminate the counterfeit voices so that the authentic voice of the Holy Spirit can be identified. As we become very familiar with the authentic, we automatically recognize the counterfeit.

Each of us has an built-in radar system that is activated more and more as we walk with God. It can become confused or blunted through lack of use and also through allowing too much access to the many voices.

Healthy relationships with God and man keep us connected to truth.

Our default position is to be in intimate fellowship with our God. In Genesis 1:26, God said, "Let us make man in our image and likeness." We are sons and daughters of the living God and as such are created to walk and talk with him, to know his voice and respond to it.

Relationship alone, however, is not enough to ensure that we can stay in a place of safety where we are not deceived and confused by those many voices.

Obedience to God and submission to godly authority also keeps us protected from deception.

Mankind was trusted with dominion and commanded to walk in that dominion while, at the same time, maintaining his position as a friend of God.

God's only requirement was that he not eat of one tree out of the many in the garden. God required active obedience to prove that man would choose to walk as his son from his free will and not as a robot that had no choice.

Obedience has no value unless there is the opportunity to disobey.

Adam and Eve walked and talked with God, shared the heart of God, and heard his voice *clearly*.

It was their disobedience in eating of the tree that separated them from God's presence and his voice and blocked their spiritual radar.

During times of war, it is the goal of our enemies to block both supply lines and communication lines. Because Adam failed to obey God and let his relationship with Eve come between him and God's voice, he was now cursed to provide for himself through hard work and would no longer have the same access to God, which he had previously enjoyed.

It is essential to value intimacy with God. Intimate relationship causes us to hear the secrets of God; his voice is clear to us because nothing comes between us

Intimacy produces revelation, that is, the secrets that are told to special friends. Intimacy is developed through time spent in the word, strategic prayer time, a heart of worship, and submission to the lordship of Christ.

We are a spirit and God is a spirit. We hear him in our spirit, through his spirit; yet our minds and belief systems, our emotions and fears, can block that voice.

Idolatry

The enemy tries to make us idolize people, or gifts that people possess, especially the prophetic gifts and creative arts. This causes us to dethrone Jesus as Lord and enthrone relationships and gifts. In turn, this causes us to draw back from that intimacy with Jesus.

The depth of our obedience is evidence of the depth of our relationship—Jesus said, "You are my friends if you do what I say."

Listening to another voice instead of God produced doubt about God's voice and distracted Adam and Eve from what God had actually said. God's words were distorted and twisted by the serpent.

The voice of the enemy will accuse God and cast doubt on both his word and his character when he said, "Has God really said that?" When you are confused about God's voice, go back to what you know God has said to you in his written and spoken word to you (Genesis 3:1). This will bring clarity to both your mind and your spirit and create a healthy filter to separate truth and error.

Guard what you look at or listen to carefully

Looking at the serpent caused Eve to listen to a lie; what we look at opens doors to wrong voices. After looking at the serpent and listening to his words, both Adam and Eve released their dominion and their relationship with God to that enemy.

Counterfeit voices come in camouflage; Satan appears as an angel of light, not in a form that would cause us to turn away from him. Our enemies camouflage and hide their troops and weapons. Their goal is destruction; they always give out counterintelligence and false information.

The counterfeit appeals to our soul and the soul's voice blocks God's voice.

The counterfeit is always based on truth and has elements of truth within it, is a small amount of truth wrapped in deception and lies. The counterfeit looks real because it is designed to deceive.

Satan disguises the truth and provides us with a counterfeit version; it looks similar to truth and feels similar to truth but has no actual value. Looking at the real exposes the counterfeit.

Know the truth by revelation

Truth alone does not free us, but revelation knowledge of the truth enables us to compare what the voice, which speaks to us, is saying to what God has said to us in the past and what his word says.

Jesus said, "I am the way, the truth, and the life . . . thief comes to rob steal, kill, and destroy." The counterfeit brings death, confusion (John 8:32).

Deception wants to steal our birthright, which is a two-way communication with God and dominion over the works of the enemy.

The counterfeit manifests as the following:

Unauthorized knowledge—"Then the LORD God took the man and put him in the Garden of Eden to tend and keep it. ¹⁶And the LORD God commanded the man, saying, "Of every tree of the garden you may freely eat; ¹⁷but of the tree of *the knowledge* of good and evil you shall not eat, for in the day that you eat of it you shall surely die" (Genesis 2:16).

We should not seek for knowledge that God does not want to give us or seek it from sources that he has forbidden.

Unauthorized knowledge gives us power, which makes us independent of God. God wants us to receive what he desires to give us and allow him to truly be the Lord of our lives. We know in part and prophesy in part until that which is perfect is come, with out the complete picture, and we should not seek for all knowledge, just that which God desires to reveal to us. [1 Corinthians 13:9]

It is important when operating in the prophetic to stay within the boundaries of revelation that comes easily to us. If we reach too deeply into the spirit realm seeking knowledge, we may access knowledge that we are not equipped to handle or that the person we are ministering to cannot handle.

Times and seasons and our own journey determine how we respond to the word of the Lord, and God alone knows when it is right for us to have that knowledge. The enemy has access to a certain amount of knowledge about people's lives and also has no concern for their well-being, so when supernatural knowledge is sought from the wrong sources (the demonic) the knowledge may be accurate but also destructive to the people concerned.

Illegitimate worship

We were created to worship and our default position is worship. If we don't worship the true God, we will worship the counterfeit god. The angels worship; heaven is full of worship and always was. As the original worship leader, Lucifer now seeks to draw worship to himself from whatever source possible. He deceives people and creates counterfeit idols to draw that worship to him.

God clearly commanded his people to worship no other gods and to place him first (Exodus 20:3).

The enemy *camouflages* modern gods as movies, books, New Age practices, and music stars so that we will not be aware that we have been drawn into idolatry.

Our culture establishes what is acceptable to worship; it is important for all Christians and especially prophetic people to resist the cultural pressure to place people or possessions or any other thing on a throne in our lives. God will dethrone those idols in our lives so that he alone can be on the throne of our lives. What we worship is determined by our ability to separate truth and deception. We see this worship in the adulation of public figures based on their gift or position in society.

When such a person dies, we see extremes of grief as people in fact grieve for what the death of that person represents—the loss of that which they worshipped and depended upon for their own comfort.

Worship that should go to the true God is transferred and stolen from him and then given to the counterfeit god. The enemy wants us to worship him or what he has created.

Pull down strongholds of the mind and emotions (2 Corinthians 10:5).

Strongholds are those ideas and beliefs that exalt themselves against the word of God by disagreeing with it.

To exalt means to "rise up against"; this is frontline spiritual warfare. The carnal mind will exalt itself and disagree with God. Romans 8:6 in the Amplified Bible says, "The mind of the flesh is sense and reason without the Holy Spirit."

Our natural mind always disagrees with the written word of God and will also disagree with the *rhema* word of God. The battle for the mind must be won continually; it is not a one-off battle but a daily event. Whenever the prophetic stirs, the mind will also speak. I still have to deal with what my mind would like to say about the prophetic words I give, even after many years of experience as a prophetic minister. When we become complacent about our mind and emotions, they will start to dominate and therefore weaken and dilute the prophetic word.

The enemy presents us with something that appeals to our senses to draw our attention from God.

The fruit in the garden was good to look at and eat; it also *appealed* to their *pride*, as they played with the idea sown into their minds by the serpent: "I will know as much as God."

"So when the woman saw that the tree *was* good for food, that it *was* pleasant to the eyes, and a tree desirable to make one wise, she took of its fruit and ate." Their spiritual eyes were opened, and they saw the spirit realm and realized that they had been talking to the devil in the guise of a serpent (Genesis 3:6).

The prophet must continue to overcome destructive thoughts and temptations to indulge in pride, self-will, glory seeking, manipulation, and a love of money.

Jesus himself fought this battle in Luke 4, but he did not obey Satan's voice or yield to the offers he was given. Satan in fact did have the authority to give what he offered to Jesus because the kingdoms of the world and the glory had been delivered to him by Adam and Eve. He was offering Jesus a chance to bypass the cross. But Jesus knew that he had to go to the cross to redeem mankind. He could not settle for the power and the glory without his ultimate mission, to please his Father by restoring mankind back to the position they were created for.

God reminds us that we too must continually fight and win this battle against lust and greed and pride.

"¹⁶**For all that is in the world—the lust of the flesh [craving for sensual gratification] and the lust of the eyes [greedy longings of the mind] and the pride of life [assurance in one's own resources or in the stability of earthly things]—these do not come from the Father but are from the world [itself]**" (1 John 2:16, Amp).

Identify your calling and gift mix

One of the major pitfalls of prophetic people is that they may believe they are a prophet when in fact they do not have that calling. If while believing themselves to be a prophet they also do not understand the role and function of a New Testament prophet, their behavior will become very destructive to people, churches, and the reputation of the prophetic.

Those who are called to the office of prophet also need to understand what God requires of them in behavior, obedience, and submission.

Let's examine the Old and New Testament models of a prophet's actions and lifestyle.

In the Old Testament we see that the prophets' messages were often demonstrated by unusual actions, perhaps even actions that would be describes as crazy.

Ezekiel was told to use a sword and cut off his hair and beard, burn a third of it, throw much of it to the wind, and bind a small amount into his hem to demonstrate God's judgment. Hosea was told to marry a harlot to demonstrate Israel's unfaithfulness; Jeremiah was told to lie 390 days on one side, and then 40 days on the other. Isaiah walked naked and barefoot for three years; what courage that must have taken.

God needed to get the people's attention, and those prophets were willing to lay aside their pride and comfort to give that message. We can be grateful that God no longer asks his prophets to do such radical things; nevertheless he does ask for great sacrifice and obedience.

Most prophets did not just visit the wilderness—they lived in it. They were so different from most people they would probably have never fitted in with general society. They had a high profile and were directly connected to the reigning king. They were known and recognized, and people regularly turned to them for God's word. They carried an aura of fear around them because when they spoke people knew that judgment, or strange requests, was most likely to be coming out of their mouths.

Perhaps Namaan, who had to dip in the dirty Jordan seven times, is one of the best examples of this. Those prophets could not live in fear of man and neither can we. Jeremiah was in prison more often that out of it; he never compromised the word of the Lord no matter how it affected his personal comfort.

Daniel, who is one of the best pictures of a prophetic intercessor we have, continually risked his life to uphold truth.

John the Baptist is the forerunner and the bridge between Old and New Testament prophets, and he lived much the same type of lifestyle as his predecessors did.

Jesus as the ultimate and complete prophet modeled the true heart and mind of those who carry God's message. He live in humility, obedience, and authority over the demonic, demonstrating

miracles as his father led him to and speaking the truth without compromise, while always demonstrating sacrificial love for the people around him. Jesus changed the role model of the prophet forever, and he is now our example upon which we should base our lives and ministry (Philippians 2:5-11).

All those who carried prophetic and apostolic mantles in the early church continually obeyed God even when his directions made no sense or even seemed strange. However, they also worked as a part of a team, lived in community with the people, and were a part of the practical decision making of the church leadership.

Prophets are now a part of the fivefold ministry, not a "voice crying in the wilderness" but part of a team. They are meant to work in unity with those other ministers for the purpose of training, equipping, and activating the church. They are no longer to be lone rangers, isolated in the wilderness, although they certainly will experience isolation and wilderness experiences.

Prophets are sometimes described in scripture as false. The definition of a false prophet is one whose primary mode of operation is from

- the wrong source of revelation—demonic, not the Holy Spirit
- the wrong motives—seeking fame, wealth, and power

(Ezekiel 13:9, Matthew 24:11)

The fruit of a false prophet is always

- confusion
- drawing people away from God and to themselves
- undisciplined and non-accountable lifestyles

A prophet who is not a false prophet may nevertheless be influenced by their soul, the demonic, the desire for fame and wealth and power, or any combination of these; however, these things are not their primary mode of operation.

All prophets are on a journey toward maturity, just as every other Christian is, and the degree of maturity achieved will determine the purity of their revelation. By removing those things that defile or clutter our discernment and spiritual ears, we make room for increased accuracy and impact to flow through us and facilitate God's will upon the earth.

While Old Testament prophets were required to be infallible to authenticate their gift, New Testament prophets are judged by their fruit. Jesus said that by their fruit we would know them.

Eternal fruit, which will remain, is only produced through the power of the Holy Spirit in our lives, our personal relationship with God, and the amount of freedom we give him to work within us.

Fruit and gifting must be balanced in our lives for the maturing of both the gift and the person carrying the gift. God does not remove gifts when people fall short of his standards. He may even continue to anoint that gift because the anointing is upon the gift and the word; sooner or later, however, God will withdraw his grace until there is repentance.

The quality and accuracy of a gift cannot be the standard by which a person is judged, as it is not God's standard of judgment. He comes and looks at the fig tree and will cause it to die if it does not bear fruit. He waits for the appropriate season, that time when fruit should appear; he gives us grace and time to change but will not always have patience when we continually fail to produce the fruit of his spirit in our lives and ministries (Luke 6:44).

Strong and accurate gifting needs to be married to a humble, teachable spirit and a positive encouraging attitude in the life of the prophet.

CHAPTER 6

The Prophet's Maturity and Transition

There are various levels of prophetic gifting and anointing. Even within the office of a prophet, I believe there are also different levels of governmental authority. There are certainly different operations or methods, if you like, in ministering the prophetic.

There can be quite a complex gift mix within a prophets' life as there can be for all Christians, and God appears to have specifically charged individuals with assignments that are geographical and people group based. Geographical assignments may be for life or a set time, but usually people groups are for life.

It is possible that a prophet will move in and out of different areas of ministry during different seasons of their lives. Sometimes the anointing to minister in a certain way will lift, and if the anointing and grace is gone for that ministry, then it is better to leave it alone.

For instance, I used to do a great deal of individual restoration ministry, just loved to do it and had no ambition to do anything else. God eventually transitioned me primarily into platform ministry and leadership within the local church. When this started happening, the grace for the long individual sessions of counseling evaporated.

When transition is occurring, there are many gray areas, and it is hard to get guidance. Certainly many of the old ways in which we have found guidance in the past will become like a dried-up well. God will seem to be totally silent. It then becomes impossible to get a prophetic word that will shed light on the future, even from previously tried and tested prophetic voices.

The road map is changing, and it is good to proceed slowly with any decisions, feeling each step and continually and keeping an open heart to the Holy Spirit to let you know if you are moving into areas that he does not want you in.

Times and seasons that are initiated by God are more fluid than those that we establish. God's seasons depend upon the actions and responses of those who are connected to our future, our own responses and actions, and his own big-picture plan for our church, region, or nation. Because we all have a role to play in God's plan, sometimes another person's failure to obey will slow down our future. This will not be able to completely abort God's plans; God always has a way of escape and, if necessary, an alternate pathway to our destiny. He alone knows when it is time to activate that alternate plan, and it is essential to walk in faith in these seasons.

Some people are assigned to specific nations or groups of nations, some to individual churches or groups of churches.

Some people carry a prophetic mantle with an apostolic edge to it, and some apostles are more prophetic than others although all apostles are very prophetic.

We cannot transition to the new until the old has been completed.

Steps to transition in the prophetic

1. Purify your gift

The soul will always contend with the spirit for dominance. They are in a war until Jesus returns, and there is no other area of gifting that will receive a greater challenge from our souls than the prophetic. The ability to hear God's voice and impart what he says accurately to others, at the correct time and with the correct attitude, is not a science but an art form.

As we allow the Holy Spirit to speak to us about our own lives and also allow mature and trusted advisors to speak to us, we start to reach that position of spiritual sonship in which we ourselves walk and talk as mature ministers of his word.

As I have previously discussed, the areas of love of money, glory, and power are major stumbling blocks in every Christian's life and in the life of the prophet and will also become a stumbling block to others.

Balaam demonstrates the fruit of a prophet who has not allowed the purification of his motives and desires, and therefore, he was nearly drawn into cursing God's people. He had a reputation as someone who could be called upon to curse, and we see that Balak, the heathen king, tried to purchase his services in this capacity. It is interesting to note that even when God told him explicitly not to go with the representatives of the king, Balaam could not accept that direction and was tempted by the wealth and power offered to him. He repeatedly asked God for permission to go until finally God released him (Numbers 22).

In the book of Psalms, we are told God gave the children of Israel what they asked for but sent leanness to their souls. It is better to obey God and go through whatever furnace or wilderness he has you in than to request or demand or try to pray your way out of that place so that your soul will feel satisfied.

Balaam had gone into such a place of deception that he could not see the angel of the Lord standing before him. Rebellion and disobedience opens the door to deception in our lives, and God requires his prophets to walk a narrow path close to him so that we do not go into rebellion and disobedience and deception. Three times, God put Balaam and his donkey in a narrow place, even allowing his foot to be crushed, the symbol of an inability to move forward. In the end he had to supernaturally reveal himself to Balaam because of the spiritual blindness that Balaam had allowed around his life.

Finally Balaam sees that he cannot curse God's people. It seems, however, that the root cause of his problem was never dealt with because ultimately he leads God's people into Baal worship and is then put to death by those same people.

The willingness to compromise diverted him from the fullness of his purpose.

If we don't deal with sin when it is the size of a snake, it eventually becomes a dragon and destroy us. In the Garden of Eden, Satan was a snake on the ground; in the book of Revelation, he is a rampaging dragon. What we feed will grow and develop a life of its' own.

2. Know your current sphere of authority

There are three main areas that God speaks to us about:

- **The local spirit realm**
  We may read the spirit realm by just picking up what is happening around us. Not everything we pick up is meant to be spoken about. Sometimes the prophet

needs to ask God to separate and refine their spiritual radar. We should not be slammed by every voice and atmosphere that is around us. The enemy likes to jam our spiritual radar by bombarding us with many thoughts, ideas, and dreams so that we use energy separating the wheat from the chaff.

This is particularly true about dreams. When we are asleep, we need to have our subconscious mind guarded by the Holy Spirit. It is good to pray every night that the only dreams that come will be those that God wants us to dream.

- **Our own lives**

We may hear things in the spirit that God is telling us personally but which are not for sharing.

When the angel appeared to Mary to tell her she would bear the Messiah, she kept all those things in her heart. Sharing prematurely can open us up to demonic attack, and our dream can even be delayed or aborted. In the early stages of pregnancy, many women do not tell of their condition until the first three months are past, the time when the risk of miscarriage is the greatest.

Joseph shared his dream about his brothers bowing down to him and found himself in a pit and then on his way to slavery, without even the chance to talk to his father. Imagine the grief in his heart as he went from being his father's favorite to not even seeing his father. God's plan for Joseph was sovereign and would come to pass in spite of his mistakes, but no doubt Joseph went through much more suffering than he needed to before this happened.

Joseph was an integral part of God's big-picture plan for his people; if he had totally walked away from God and His purposes, then God would have released someone else to take his place. God is never without a backup plan. He has linked his purposes to the will of his people, and our willingness to work with him is essential to his purposes.

When he finally saw his brothers again many years later, he needed to be alone to express his profound grief, which he had carried for many years. God will often take us back to old hurts so that they can receive some more healing before we enter a new season.

At one stage of my life, I felt a strong urge to go back and visit the places where I had spent most of my childhood. I was not conscious of needing any more emotional healing but was surprised that as I visited these old places, some previously unknown issues surfaced, and I was able to take them to God for healing. It was shortly after this that God expanded my ministry greatly.

- **The lives of others and the churches and regions, which God gives us responsibility for**
This can start in a very small way, and it is important to use whatever revelation you have, as this will cause the gift to grow. In my own life, I started to receive scripture along with a strong sense of God's presence, and I would share those scriptures with the small group I fellowshipped in. Soon I could tell who the scripture was for, and then I started to get a sentence. My first prophecy was only four words long. I said to the woman next to me, "God is your provider." I had no

idea that her husband had lost his job the previous day. She broke down sobbing, as she saw that God knew and cared about their dilemma.

I progressed quickly to ministering at leaders' retreats and within my local church. From the beginning I was very accurate; it seemed my gift had been hidden even to me until suddenly it appeared and grew very quickly. I was about forty years old when this started to happen.

As my reputation grew, God opened doors for me to minister in other churches, and I began to receive revelation for the churches and the regions they were in.

International ministry opened up to me, and I learned to deal with regional principalities and powers. This could only be done because God himself had called and anointed me for this task. It was not something I sought after but something God not only called me to. He had to put quite a lot of pressure on me to step into.

I was not naturally inclined to leave the comforts of home, and God reminded me one day of a word that had been given to me by a man I really respected: "Ask me for the nations." That was all that was said, but it was a true word from the Lord; and so, fairly reluctantly, I started to ask God for the nations. It was not very long at all after I started to pray that prayer that I was given a ticket to England and all of my original international contacts opened up through that one trip.

Our cooperation with God's plan produces eternal fruit.
Not all prophetic people and not all prophets are called to one nation or to many nations. Some are

called to full-time prayer, ministry in the marketplace, or local church ministry. It is very important indeed to stay within the calling that God has upon your life; it is only within that boundary that we can prosper.

3. Recognise your Transition time from the gift to the office

There is a process in the life of the prophet where God releases them to operate as a prophet and not just within the boundaries of the gift of prophecy. This can be a difficult time, as usually the prophet's degree and quality of revelation is far greater than what they can and should deliver until they are released by God and also by their spiritual authorities to do so.

One of the signs of a prophet's mantle is that other fivefold ministries recognize and acknowledge that mantle, and as this starts to happen, it is important to continually check our spirits to make sure we are moving with the spirit of God and not running ahead of him.

This started to happen for me sometime after God has spoken to me about my calling. My own pastors and other leaders started to call me a prophet, and for the first time, I received a prophetic word from a visiting ministry that I was a prophet.

If we reverse this order, acting on a prophesy or what God has said to us without waiting for the acknowledgment by our authorities, we step outside of the protection of God's authority structure, and this will open us up to demonic attack.

The gift does make room for its operation, and when the time is right, God will give the recognition that is needed.

Jesus acknowledged the role of John the Baptist as a prophetic voice, first by asking John to baptize him (Matthew 1:13) and then by speaking about his role publicly (Matthew 11:11).

The apostles in the early church publicly acknowledged and laid hands upon leaders and also discipled them in their roles.

Once again, the scriptural picture of the function of a prophet in this dispensation is that of a team member working with and under authority. This produces a dynamic of increased and multiplied power, which pushes back the gates of hell.

During the time of transition into the office of prophet I have found it is better to go slowly, write down words, and submit them to the church pastor before giving them. It is also helpful to slow down your speech so that you do not allow directive words out of your mouth, and be careful if you have direction to wrap it around with words such as "I feel" or "please take this to your pastor for their judgment."

Once there is a maturity in the office of prophet, with hopefully some wisdom and experience, then there can be a gradual release of words that contain the fullness of revelation. It is important not to lose sight of the fact that God loves his people and his church, and even when he rebukes and corrects, he will do it in love.

There should always be a redemptive factor in prophecy; the answer should be provided along with any correction.

Joseph spent many years in prison, falsely accused in a foreign land. He would have had much opportunity to brood and become bitter. In some way, he allowed God to minister to him so that his heart was sweet and he became a part of the answer in prison, interpreting dreams and producing sweet fruit to others. When the time came that he was publicly acknowledged as a prophet and was called before Pharaoh, he had an opportunity to pay Pharaoh back for his years of unjust imprisonment.

He could have chastised Pharaoh, condemning him and delivering the interpretation of the dream about a severe famine as a judgment against him. What he actually did was interpret the dreams accurately, but he also provided the answer through a word of wisdom. He told Pharaoh to build barns and store the excess crop to be used during the famine.

The negative alone will destroy, and a mature prophetic person will seek for the redemptive factor in a word. God always provides a way out, a way of escape; and very, very rarely would it be necessary to deliver a word that was all about the punishment or the consequences.

Delivering judgmental words is not a sign of being a prophet; it is always easier to see the negative, but that is sometimes a sign of immaturity and lack of understanding of the grace factor.

It is the Holy Spirit's role to convict of sin and judgment and righteousness (John 16:8). It is sometimes the role of the prophet to speak words that the Holy Spirit can work with; it is not necessary to try and produce conviction, as the Holy Spirit will do this even without the knowledge of the person who is prophesying.

All gifts start out as a seed; and that seed needs planting, nurturing, and training. Sometimes the Master Gardener transplants that little plant as it outgrows its position or needs a change of environment. The plant itself should not decide when to move or change but leave that decision to the gardener. Jesus is our master gardener, and he will supervise the growth of our gifts. The prophetic is a tender plant and needs special attention because of its power to do great good and great destruction.

We have the responsibility to submit our gifts to God, who gave them, and obey him constantly. Sometimes he will ask us to do specific training as Timothy was told to study to show himself approved for the ministry. Sometimes God just releases us into his school.

There are certain guidelines given to us in scripture that we can place around our gift, like a safety rail, which will produce healthy fruit and which will leave a beautiful fragrance of Christ as we minister.

4. Emphasize the positive

Criticism is not a work of the spirit but a manifestation of the flesh. The difference between criticism and discernment is the attitude and motivation of the person speaking. The role of the prophetic at any level is to give answers, vision, and wisdom.

To see the problem without giving a constructive answer is to create more of a problem than was originally there.

It is necessary to understand that the operation of the prophetic in the Old Testament is different from its operation in the New Testament because we are now in the dispensation of grace. God can and does speak to individual Christians, and it is now the Holy Spirit's role to convict of sin and judgment. Not ours. God will use our words, but we should not deliver words in a judgmental spirit. We are not required to be judge, jury, and executioner; we are only required to speak the words God says (John 16:7).

When a prophet speaks, they can be speaking in a positive way, and the Holy Spirit can take that message and reveal those things that are not actually being said to the individual hearing them.

Rarely indeed would it be necessary to deliver public judgment. Many times I have spoken prophetically to individuals; and God, who knows all about that person, has convicted them of sin, which I had not seen, let alone spoken about to them.

One of the main vulnerabilities of the prophet is a tendency to see only the negative or to major on the negative.
It takes maturity to see the negative and turn it into a positive.
It was after forty years in a foreign land and many years unjustly accused in prison in that land that Joseph could stand before Pharaoh to interpret his dream and not only give him the interpretation but also a wise solution to his problem. He did not just affirm the problem; he provided the answer.

5. Know your scriptural boundaries

A prophet is released to operate in a different set of boundaries than those who operate the prophetic gift. One of the main vulnerabilities of the prophet is a tendency to see only the negative or to major on the negative.

They are released to activate gifts, rebuke, correct, and set ministries apart.

One of the main differences between the gift of prophecy and the office of prophet is the impact created by a prophet's words.

Some people operate the prophetic gift regularly, often at a very high level of accuracy.

The gift is given to

- edify (*oikodomeo*): to be a house builder, renew and refresh
- exhort (*parakaleo*): comfort, console
- comfort (*paramuthia*): to encourage someone who is weary under pressure or afflictions (1 Corinthians 12:10)
- those who are recognized prophets may give direction and correction (Acts 11:27,28)

The gift is available for everyone. In fact, we are told to desire to prophecy but to pursue love. The foundation of all prophetic ministry needs to be love (1 Corinthians 14:1).

Some people operate the prophetic gift regularly, often at a very high level of accuracy, but still need to operate within the boundaries of the gift of prophecy (1 Corinthians 12:10).

God has placed a complete chapter about love in the midst of Paul's teachings on spiritual gifts and their operation in the church. Without love all the gifts are as nothing, and prophecy in particular becomes destructive unless the person operating it has a love for people in general and a concern for their welfare.

To desire prophecy means to long for, crave, or yearn for; but we are told to pursue love, which means to chase or hunt it down.

Love for people and a recognition of the fact that people are valuable to God will automatically put a safety rail around what we say.

Prophets and prophetic people need to ask God to give them his love for the people.

Wisdom and timing is essential for healthy prophetic function.

There is an old saying that says you can't judge a book by its cover. There is a lot of truth in this, but at the same time, the way we present ourselves and our gift will open or close the hearts of the people. I am not talking about compromising the truth of what God says to us but about discerning timing and understanding the wisdom of presenting the word of the Lord in such a way that we are working with the Holy Spirit and not against him.

Hearing from God is relatively simple; separating his voice from other voices can be learned through experience, but the area where most people fail to reach maturity and therefore grow their mantle is in timing and methodology.

God asks us to

- receive the message
- deliver the message
- let the Holy Spirit interpret the message

It is important to consider the outworking of the prophetic as it flows through our lives.

There are certain perspectives on how the prophetic should operate, which color presentation methods and can do great damage to the people receiving prophecy.

For instance,

I must speak what I see and hear even when it is negative.

Revelation comes in many ways, which are determined by our own listening style, our personalities, and our gift mix. Some hear a still small voice, some see pictures or dream, some receive revelation through scripture, some will, at different times, hear God in all of these ways. Occasionally, God speaks through an audible voice.

The way we hear is not important except in the sense of the importance of recognizing God's voice in whichever way it comes; what we do with that revelation is what determines the outcome.

It is a myth to believe that just because we have seen and heard in the spirit, we have to speak about it. If we do not need to speak about it, it may be because there is often a timing factor to be considered, or perhaps God has shown us a need so that we will pray about it.

We receive the message, ask God how and when we should deliver the message, and then allow the Holy Spirit to interpret it.

One of the reasons that God puts the prophets through such immense training is to remove from their souls the dysfunctions that would cause them to base their identity upon their gifts.

When our identity is obtained from our gift, then, of course, we have a compulsive need to be always right; otherwise, our identity is compromised.

The golden rule of prophecy is that God has given us control of when and how we express it.

We see this expressed in the word of God:

The spirits of the prophets are under the speakers control and subject to being silenced as may be necessary (1 Corinthians 14:32, Amp).

A mature prophetic expression should come as a *rhema* word with all unnecessary "fill-in" words cut out of it.

The rhema *word is a revealed portion of the word of God or a specific word for a specific person*

One of the reasons God puts his prophets through such immense training processes is to remove from their souls the weaknesses, hurts, mind-sets, and immaturities that would distort or defile his words through them.

We are created to hear from God, and sometimes we just automatically read the spirit realm; we have not necessarily received a message that we should deliver. It takes wisdom and experience to determine what to do with the message and when to deliver it.

Mary pondered the revelation that she would be the mother of the Messiah in her heart (Luke 2:19).

God shares the secret things of his heart with those who walk closely with him; he speaks to the prophets first. Often that information does not apply to the present but to the future. I have personally found that much of what God shows me is at least two years ahead of its fulfillment.

Seeing and hearing the negative is always easier than seeing and hearing the positive. If you see a problem or anything negative, first pray about it. If the burden cannot be released through prayer, then take it to a pastor or elder for their judgment and action and leave it with them.

I am a prophet and therefore am always right.

If you believe you are or must always be right, then you make yourself unavailable for correction. Certainly a prophet should be highly accurate; it is one of the distinguishing features of the prophetic office, but no one is infallible. The Bible says we see in part and know in part. There is a scriptural requirement for all prophecy to be judged, especially by their peers in the New Testament church: "Let the prophets speak and let the others [prophets] judge" (1 Corinthians 14:29).

Old Testament prophets had to be totally accurate or face stoning, but this is not the case in this dispensation. Because we are in the dispensation of grace and also because there are many more prophets now who can bring different aspects of what God is saying. God also speaks to all his people, and there is a requirement upon each individual to take responsibility for their own decision by developing their own ability to hear God. The Holy Spirit is our teacher and our inner judge (Deuteronomy 18:20-22).

A prophet has authority over local church pastors.

Local church pastors have particular responsibility to protect their people—they "watch for their souls" (Hebrews

13:7)—and because of this, the senior pastor is responsible to God for the state of their sheep; and the prophet, whether visiting or resident, must submit to that authority. The other fivefold ministries together with the prophet and the pastor support, build, and serve the local church and its pastor.

Authority issues must be clearly established in the heart of the prophet.

There is divine order in correctly used authority, which allows blessing to flow.

(Psalms 133:2)
Jesus obeyed his father . . . (John 3:34, Luke 4:13, Romans 5:12, 21 Philippians 2:1-9)
Individuals obey God . . . (James 4:7)
Children obey parents . . . (Ephesians 6:1, Colossians 3:18-22)
Wives obey husbands . . . (Ephesians 5:22)
Servants obey magistrates . . . (Titus 3:1)
Christians obey their leaders . . . (Hebrews 13:17)

Like all principles that God has established for our blessing, obedience has been distorted and abused by the enemy; and because of this, we tend to see it as control, even when it is not. Align yourself with godly authorities and ask God to clarify your discernment so that you will recognize true control and be able to separate yourself from it.

Prophetic Protocols

Deliver the message with credibility

The normal and everyday expression of prophetic revelation is just as powerful, if not more so than a spooky ethereal presentation. We can and should use everyday language and expressions relevant to our own culture, and we see that Jesus used examples in his parables about everyday activities of the culture around him. Including scripture lends a great deal of power to the word from God, and God will use what we have stored within our hearts of his word to speak to people.

Prophetic revelation can be delivered in a conversational tone of voice, and it is usually better to minimize emotional expressions, as this can be a great distraction from what God is saying.

Wording can be changed or adjusted to wisely express the heart of God. A seasoned prophetic minister can do this in a skillful way without losing what God wants to say. It is better to prophesy the answer, for example, rather than tell someone you see pride in their lives. Prophesy to them about the work of humility God is doing in their lives; it gives the same message in a way that is easier for people to receive and opens up the healing power of God to release them from pride.

Sometimes strong words and direct rebukes may be necessary, but it is important to feel the heart of God for the person you are ministering to, as God alone knows the best way to send his word out.

Be cautious about singing prophecy unless you have the anointing and the voice to do this well; it will only distract from the message. Don't expect that your word has to be long and involved to be effective; some of the most impacting words I have ever given have been short.

If it is a word from God, it will be powerful and effective in whatever format God sends it. Truly even a single word or a phrase, when it comes from God's heart, can change a life.

Don't keep repeating yourself while trying to hear the next thing God wants to say; repetition is only effective if God is empowering it. If it is too hard to hear anymore, then simply stop.

What do I do with my personal prophetic word?

Most people have received words that have not yet come to pass. Sometimes this is because it is not yet God's timing, but we have a responsibility to do whatever we need to, to release those words so that when the time is right they will be activated.

Some keys to activate your personal words:

Compare it to others you have received, look for a common theme, and then pray about the common theme. God is clearly sending you a message when he repeats himself.

Obey any instructions that God has given you from any reliable source. Declare your prophecy out loud, thanking God for the fulfillment of his word.

Do warfare with your prophecy; use it as a sword that God has given you to overcome the opposing circumstances, which will rise up against that word when it is given. The enemy likes to kill the word at its birth and will certainly cause the opposite to happen initially.

If you believe it is a word from God then don't back down, but keep pressing in to receive it in faith.

The fulfillment of all prophetic words are conditional upon our obedience in all areas of life, whether that is stated in the prophecy or not.

Don't speak negatives about your word. Saying you can't do it or don't want to, you can pull it down and stop its fulfillment. If you are unsure of any part of it, just keep it and wait for God to confirm it.

Submit it to those in authority over you for their counsel.

Chapter 7

The Prophet and the Church

One of the most difficult areas for the prophet to work in can be the local church, but it is also the most necessary for the maturing and stability of the prophet. Being based in a local church and also in accountable relationship with local church authorities places protection around the life and the mantle of the prophet.

An accountable relationship is one where the prophet is personally known to the church leaders and is willing to share their struggles with those leaders and receive input.

The prophet, whether visiting or locally based, does not have a mandate to control, intimidate, or overrule the church authorities. All fivefold gifts have equal value and governmental authority but have different roles and functions, and they were created to form a team that builds the local church.

God will place a prophet in a church for the benefit of that church; unfortunately not all pastors are willing to allow that prophet to operate in the role that would build the church.

The relationships between pastors and prophets can be very tense and difficult, but when they are worked through in a godly way, they can become very fruitful for both parties.

Sometimes a pastor is afraid of damage to the flock occurring because of the words and actions of prophetic people. This is quite a legitimate fear, as truly much damage has been done to the sheep through alleged prophets who have operated out of their flesh in a spirit of harshness and judgment.

It is the pastors' role to shepherd the flock, to protect and nurture the sheep, and to keep the wolves away, even if they are in sheep's clothing. The analogy of a wolf being in sheep's clothing expresses the idea of someone who has become known and accepted by the people and so can do more damage from within.

People with prophetic gifting may either come in openly declaring themselves to be sent from God to minister to the church, or they may present as just one of the sheep, win the friendship of the people, and then start to operate prophetically in a damaging way.

Perhaps one of the greatest advantages I received as I grew into the prophet's mantle was that I initially worked in the pastoral role in the churches I was based in, counseling and teaching and shepherding people. This enabled me to see the pastors' perspective and to have a protective attitude toward the flock of God.

I believe that all prophetically gifted people, no matter how great their calling, should grow up into that mantle by serving in the house of God. Samuel was placed in the temple as a child and was in the role of a servant who was training to be a priest/prophet.

The local church provides a stone-upon-stone dynamic. We are likened to living stones all placed to build the house of God. A stone needs to be shaped so that it will fit smoothly and safely in its right place next to the other stones. When stones are correctly placed and shaped, the wall holds together without mortar. All over the UK and Europe, there are stone fences that have held together for centuries by the shaping and positioning alone.

Stone buildings, which of course have a far greater height than fences and must hold the weight of a roof, are joined with mortar; but the shaping and positioning are just as important.

I believe that the mortar can be likened to the love we are called to have for each other. This love covers a multitude of sins; it does not conceal sin, which should be revealed, but it makes allowance for the weakness of the people and loves them just as they are.

This love is an essential element in the working relationship of the senior pastor and the prophet. There must be a mutual godly love and respect, an allowance and understanding of the weaknesses in the other person, a willingness to listen to the point of view of the other, and a respect that has been earned for their respective roles.

The role of a person who is called, placed, and recognized as a prophet in a local church is to:

1. Flow with and come under the authority structure of the local church

This can prove very challenging for the prophet, especially if they also operate an itinerant ministry, as they are usually given a great deal of authority and freedom to operate when they visit a church. Within their own church, however, the gift must be contained within the Sunday structure of a meeting and the working relationship with the other church leaders, which allows for input from everyone being of equal value, even when they have the full endorsement of the pastor to operate their gifting.

The prophet must have been broken and pruned by God to submit with a right heart to this. Within the local church, the prophet voluntarily lays down their own vision to the vision of the local church family. The prophet must be able to accept that their revelation will not necessarily be acted upon within their own church. They are like the postman whose role it is to deliver the mail, not to wait and see that it is opened and acted upon. This takes a lot of grace and humility and a constant dying to their own will.

2. Direct the people to the senior pastor's leadership

The prophetic mantle carries the power of attraction, and it is often the case that people will follow a prophet because of the mystery and the strong sense of God's power and presence that a prophet carries, not to mention the enticement of the prophetic word.

A pastor wields the shepherd's rod, which protects but also corrects; and so as children will rebel against their parents and listen to their peers, God's children are vulnerable to rebelling against the pastor and following the prophet.

The prophet therefore must understand God's principles of authority very well and not allow people to follow them in a way that take away the pastor's authority.

When criticism of the pastor is brought to the prophet, they must not enter into a critical spirit but direct the people to resolve those conflicts in a scriptural way. If this is not done, an Absalom spirit can start to operate through the life of the prophet.

The prophet's mantle must not be used to seduce the people; this is witchcraft as we see it demonstrated in the word through Absalom (Samuel 15:1, 2).

It is easy for a prophet to become proud and seek to draw people after themselves because of the amount of adulation many people give them because of their gift. If the prophet allows the people to idolize them, God will judge them very harshly indeed. It would be easy to be tempted to use that gift to overthrow or undermine the pastor's authority; this is why the pruning and shaping of God is so essential in the life of the prophet. A constant death to their own desires becomes necessary.

A prophet must have a heart for the sheep as Jesus the greatest prophet, who is also the greatest shepherd, has.

3. Add to the growth of the church and its people

The prophet's mantle is usually manifested with teaching or preaching gifts, sometimes with a training gift, a counseling gift, or perhaps also the power gift of miracles.

These manifestations work very well on the platform and in an itinerant mode, but they can also produce great fruit if directed in the local church into training opportunities. Reproduction and discipleship are an essential element of all Christian growth and even more so for those with a fivefold calling. The prophet must come down out of the ethereal and allow their gifts to be reproduced as much as possible in others by making that gifting available to the people in their local church in a hands-on application format.

This may mean overseeing small groups, personal meetings for the purpose of counseling or discipleship, or implementing training schools.

The mission of all Christians to reach the lost for Christ must not be forgotten, and the prophetic can certainly be used to minister to the unsaved. When they hear the heart of God toward them through the prophetic, many will come to Jesus immediately.

The pastor's role toward the prophet is to:

1. **Nurture and encourage prophetic ministry within the church while keeping healthy boundaries**

   We do not usually throw our babies away because they are messy, smelly, and demanding; that is the behavior we expect of them and we bear with it while, at the same time, training them to behave in a more acceptable way. Emerging prophets need the loving and positive support of a wise pastor who will release their gift while also training them in character development.

2. **Provide and require training for emerging prophets**

   A clear and approved training pathway will encourage a prophet and make them feel that their gift is recognized and welcome in the house. Although some may leave, declaring this to be controlling, those with a right heart will submit to this process. It is important for the pastor to understand just how grueling it can be to the soul of a prophet to submit to boundaries and training, when they primarily like to work in the spirit realm. They will be very focused on hearing and processing revelation and are not always easy to direct into practical areas.

3. **Communicate clearly and listen attentively to their insights**

   Communication is a major element in the prophet's life. They need to feel that they have been heard and that what they say is being weighed and seriously considered. They already have to deal with the frustrations of misunderstanding from those who do not see in the spirit as they do; the least they need is to know that the pastor will take them seriously and listen to them often, hearing their heart, vision, and personal frustrations.

They love to feel heard and will get frustrated and angry if they think you don't take their revelation seriously. Emphasize your appreciation of them as people, and assure them that you will pray about what they have said.

4. Show understanding of the training process that they go through

This training is long and hard for those called to the office of prophet. Those with other giftings will often see fruit and progress long before the prophet sees it. Although the emerging prophet may sound and even be overly negative about their experiences, it is important to take what they say seriously even though it may also be necessary to help them to focus on what is positive in their lives. Acknowledgment of their pain helps to build a platform for constructive input into their lives.Respect needs to be shown for the price a prophet pays to develop their gift.

It is important for the pastor to have some understanding of the development process of a prophet; many of them have been through deep grief and tragic circumstances, and they may have come through deep rejection from church authorities in other places. Perhaps this rejection came because of their own immature behavior, or perhaps it has come because of the fears and lack of understanding of those authorities. Whatever the reason, healing is needed and will come best through their own pastor.

5. **Speak to them about their errors in a loving way, extending grace**

Harsh correction will kill their revelation and vision. If you have to correct them, help them to understand that you are not rejecting them personally but "judging" their revelation. There will be times when you think they are wrong, and then they are proven to be right. If this happens, it is good to communicate this to them; it will reassure the prophet that you understand the mysterious elements of the prophetic, which do not always reveal themselves until a later time. Unless they receive regular encouragement about their accuracy, they may become so discouraged they will draw back.

6. **Evaluate their emotional health, foundational spiritual maturity, and belief systems**

If the pastor understands the present state of the prophet, they can adapt their correction and communication accordingly. There are two main areas of dysfunction, which will need evaluating in the life of the prophet.

The emerging prophets often have faulty foundations because of their personal experiences and the strong attack of the spirit realm, which recognizes their mantle early in their lives and tries to kill them either physically, mentally, emotionally, or all three. Because of this, they may have a fractured soul, which operates out of rejection, manifesting either independence or rebellion. They often battle emotional highs and lows, feelings of failure and insecurity, and may not have yet learned to recognize when they are responding to their own circumstances or their sense of the spirit realm around them.

The emerging prophets often have faulty belief systems.

If they believe that they need to model their behavior on Old Testament prophets or perhaps upon more modern ministries that have behaved in some eccentric ways, they will appear quite eccentric and unbalanced. A common belief is that if they have heard from God, then everyone must do what they say without question. They may believe that no one can correct them because of their superior ability to hear from God. These beliefs need to be addressed using scripture so that the prophet can mature in this area.

7. Provide an avenue for any emotional healing

Connect them with a support system, counselors if necessary, but also more mature prophetic people, who can mentor them in the prophetic, especially if that is not a strong gifting on the pastor's life; and also provide mentoring for them in areas of character.

8. Provide a place of ministry for them where possible

Enable them to operate their gifting, providing whatever supervision is needed while also helping them to understand that you are for them, not against them.

Alternatively, provide a place of training and healing for them until you can let them minister. Mentor them personally, if possible; a spiritual father produces after their own kind. If you want a healthy prophet, it is necessary to be a healthy parent to them.

9. Recognize the difference between immaturity and weakness

Immature prophets may appear rebellious, when in fact they are operating out of their own misunderstanding of the prophet's role or their lack of understanding of the prophet's training process and time of release. We do not and should not punish children for childish mistakes, clumsiness, or lack of emotional control appropriate to their age; but we do discipline them and train them to learn to behave in more mature ways.

Labeling a prophet rebellious when they are just immature can do great damage to the pastor's relationship with them and their personal growth. Either they will become rebellious, feeling that they have to be faithful to the call of God, rather than the controls of man, or they will suppress their gift totally and withdraw from ministry and perhaps even the church.

God himself will definitely chasten the rebellious prophet who refuses to submit to church authority and loving correction. If that prophet walks away from the church in rebellion they will truly go into a vast wilderness until they repent.

10. Release the mature prophet/prophets in the church to oversee the emerging prophets

Mature prophets will recognize rebellion and immaturity in the emerging prophets before anyone else will. Many will just look at the gift and the anointing, but a mature prophet will recognize a younger version of themselves. Their spiritual radar is sharp and tuned in to discerning the thoughts and intents of the heart of the people, especially those prophetically mantled.

Mature prophets remember the heavy lessons on submission and obedience, which God put them through repeatedly, and will also recognize when the emerging prophet is in that process. They can be an amazing source of encouragement and strength to those who will allow them to be.

11. Evaluate the impact and influence they have upon the church to establish their credentials

A mature and seasoned church prophet will be actively involved in the lives of the people. They tend to have some positive influence in every part of the church, not usually or necessarily a position of authority or leadership in every area, but the positive fruit of their presence produces harmony, reconciliation, growth, and strength in individuals and the church overall. They will always point people toward the church vision.

If their impact and fruit is not positive and not influential within the church, their heart is not knitted to the church, and they cannot function effectively as church prophets. They function instead as hirelings, whose own the sheep are not. Such people do not care for the welfare of the sheep, only for what can be obtained from them (John 10:12).

12. Face his own challenges honestly

We have spoken about the prophet's immaturity and challenges; the pastor also faces challenges when allowing the ministry of a prophet within their church. An itinerant prophet will come and go, and any errors they have made or damage they have done can be corrected by the pastor and his team.

A prophet who is released in the local church as a resident prophet, however, will automatically cause a different dynamic, as the pastor must be able to navigate their own feelings of insecurity, which may be activated by the amount of respect the prophet attracts.

An immature pastor will suppress the prophet, perhaps even make their life so difficult they will leave the church; but a mature pastor will recognize the value of that prophet's gift and not let their own feelings interfere with a healthy relationship.

If the pastor's own issues and challenges are too strong, they can become a Saul to the prophet.

The spirit of Saul is activated by jealousy and is a sort of love-hate relationship, which is very complex. On one hand the pastor will love and value the prophet; on the other hand, they hate to see the strong gifting and respect the people give to them. Sometimes the pastor will feel inadequate even when their own gifts are extremely strong. As we discussed in an earlier chapter, jealousy often rises up against the prophet; it is sad indeed when a ministry relationship breaks down under this assignment of the enemy.

The spirit of Saul will try to kill the prophet, and this can eventually drive them out of the palace as David was driven out. David had kept his heart right toward Saul and loved him in spite of the way he was treated. He left reluctantly and continued to honor Saul, refusing to kill Saul when he had the opportunity. He is a wonderful example of a prophet who behaved honorably.

Pastors need to allow the processing of the Holy Spirit also in their hearts for the harmonious working together of the gifted ministry people within their church. There is a fine line between godly discipline and structure and control, which suppress, limits, and even drives out those who God is raising up.

Fathers rejoice when their children mature and even excel them. True fathers long to see their children have more than they have had.

The role of the church prophet

The church prophet is first and foremost a sentinel and a watchman for the church. This does not conflict with the role of the senior pastor, who is primarily responsible for the church, but it is a ministry that supports the senior pastor's role

The prophet has very sensitive radar and will constantly monitor the atmosphere in the church and outside of the church. They will sense danger approaching usually before anyone else will. Part of the pressure of the prophet's mantle is this discernment, which sees the danger before others see it; they also have an acute discernment about people's motives and are often seen to be critical, when in fact they are simply operating in their gifting.

A wise pastor will understand this and not crush the prophet when they present their discernment to him but will allow for their track record and their overall accuracy in judging the information they bring. They will take such discernment, especially about people, into their consideration when planning and appointing staff and leadership.

The prophet will always uphold God's standards and his word when they see the church slipping in any way from these; they will sound an alarm.

The prophet provides prayer support and rallies others into that support role, especially in times of crisis.

The church prophet helps the church to maintain balance and recognizes when the church deviates too far into any area. Church life is a balance of inspired praise and worship and the word of God. If the word is excluded or adapted to present a politically correct message or a message that tickles the ears of the hearers, the prophet will feel God's pain and speak about it. If too much of the flesh is present in worship manifestations, the prophet's spirit will cringe; the prophet feels what God feels about this more than another person because the prophet is God's defender and spokesman.

End-time prophets and apostles

A foundation of truth, wisdom, and clear, sharp discernment of the spirit realm and its activities will be essential requirements for all Christians in the coming days. God is in the process of raising up his end-time army, and prophets and apostles will be an integral part of this army as never before seen upon the earth. The partnership of the apostle and the prophet produces an alliance of revelation, structure, and supernatural authority and power that dries back the demonic spirit realm and opens up the heavens.

The Bible teaches us that apostles and prophets are the foundation of the church; they put vision and structure around God's purposes. The spiritual marriage of apostles and prophets in a working relationship will realign churches and nations to God's purposes in the end times. God will raise up these hidden ones; some have been hidden, and some have been out of alignment, but part of the preparation for the return of Jesus Christ is and must be the raising up to visibility, honor, and recognition, those with the mantle of apostle and prophet.

There has been a dishonoring of the prophetic, and God will restore the prophetic to his original plan so that his power and his voice can be heard by the church.

The heavens are retaining Jesus until the restoration of all things (Acts 2:21). This restoration includes the Jews, Jerusalem, the temple ownership, and the balanced fivefold leadership structure of the Body of Christ.

"[19]Now, therefore, you are no longer strangers and foreigners, but fellow citizens with the saints and members of the household of God, [20]having been built on the foundation of the apostles and prophets, Jesus Christ Himself being the chief corner stone, [21]in whom the whole building, being joined together, grows into a holy temple in the Lord, [22]in whom you also are being built together for a dwelling place of God in the Spirit" (Ephesians 2:19-22, New Living).

The raising up of God's end-time prophets and apostles will help to counteract the increased voice of the enemy that seeks to distract and destroy the Body of Christ.

End-time assignments of the enemy

Jesus taught us that many of the Christians will be deceived in the end times; rebellion and independence will abound, and this opens the door to deception. Many will be offended and will break fellowship because of this offense. Spirits of offense, deception, and rebellion are released upon the earth like never before; they are like a plague that has overcome much of the Body of Christ. There is great confusion around the prophetic people, and at a time when we need to hear from God more clearly than ever, we are battling a confused atmosphere and mental pressure, which are stronger than they have ever been before.

Signs of deception (Matthew 24)

- No acknowledgement of Jesus and the work of the cross
- Puts power in the hands of people without being submitted to Christ (independence)
- Draws people's worship to their own abilities or that of others
- Draws attention to the person's gifts rather than the power of God (Acts 16:16)
- Overrides the persons will—initially or eventually
- Takes attention from what God is saying through his appointed leader

Because of the massive deception that is abounding, counterfeit prophetic gifts abound and manifest as New Age and psychic; however, within the church, Christians are vulnerable to these counterfeit gifts and need to be more careful than ever to surround their lives with people who understand the spirit realm and who will speak to them if they start to operate outside of the Holy Spirit gifting.

It is the role of the end-time prophets to expose deception and bring alignment with the word and purposes of God to the Body of Christ.

Chapter 8

Women and Prophetic Mantles

God has and does anoint women in both past generations and the present one, to carry ministry gifts of all types. The original prophetic promise to women was that they would "bruise Satan's head" (Genesis 3:15). This referred to the fact that a woman would give birth to the Messiah, but I believe it has an even greater application to the role of women who are anointed to bring freedom and healing and the power of the Holy Spirit to their generation.

The rage of the enemy has been released against women since she gave birth to Jesus, and as much as he could, he suppressed, dehumanized, and murdered women for many generations. To this day, in countries where Jesus Christ is not acknowledged as God, women are often treated as possessions and as of much less value than a man.

Women were originally created to carry spiritual authority that is equal to that of men in spiritual matters. It is only in the marriage relationship that a man should take the lead while all the time recognizing that his wife is given to him as "helper, comparable, suitable and adapted and complimentary to him" (Genesis 2:18, Amp).

The wise man will honor and recognize his wife's gifts and spiritual authority and encourage and release her to be everything that God has called her to be.

The woman is called uniquely by God to make her own decisions about salvation and obedience to him. She is given her own spiritual gifts and calling and will be required by God to give an account of them.

God has often used women to radically change situations and even national laws in the Old Testament.

Women changed the following:

- Laws of inheritance (Numbers 27:6-10, Job 42:1)
- National laws about the Jews (Esther 9:29-32)
- Esther was released by the king to write new laws about the Jews; a national festival called Purim was established and is celebrated to this day in honor of the event.

Women initiated dynamic spiritual warfare

Women like Deborah led the army in prophetic praise and warfare.

Women protected vision

A woman called Abigail, the wife of a churlish (cruel and hard-hearted) man called Nabal intervened with wisdom and courage to protect her people from the results of his foolish actions. In other words, to protect vision and future. (1 Samuel 25:1, 2).

A wise woman who is not even named spoke to king Joab and asked him not to destroy a city so that the inheritance of the Lord would be preserved (2 Samuel 20:16).

In the New Testament women demonstrated divine discernment and deep spiritual hunger.

A woman called Anna was one of the first two people to recognize who Jesus was as a baby. Women were the first to see the empty tomb, and a woman was the first person to see Jesus after his resurrection. Jesus talked to a woman about theology, a subject usually reserved for men; she was not even a Jewess but a Samaritan. Jesus also affirmed Mary's choice to sit at his feet and learn from him rather than do housework at that time. Women financed Jesus's ministry.

The apostle Paul writes of God's view of women in Galatians 2:28. "There is neither male nor female in Christ," and Jesus continually affirmed and lifted women back to their rightful place during his earthly lifetime.

Women are prophetically called to birth change and to protect and preserve life, both spiritual and natural.

God gives his prophetic call to his daughters when he says that Sarah herself received "strength to conceive seed." This was the seed of the promise, the seed of the future; women are life givers and life nurturers and have the power to give and to nurture spiritual life (Hebrews 11:11).

The Bible says we will be Sarah's daughters if we *"don't give way to hysterical fears, and do not let anxiety unnerve us"* (1 Peter 3:6).

Overcoming practical difficulties

We have seen many women rise into strong and publicly recognized ministries, teaching the word of God, ministering to the poor, and establishing strong business ventures. Women now function in high levels of natural and spiritual authority, and God is indeed reversing the curse of sin from their lives by blessing their gifts and opening doors

The difficulty for women has always been to maintain a balance between marriage and family responsibilities and also ministry responsibilities. Men also face this situation, but generally speaking, a woman will do most of the nurturing of the children and home duties, not to mention the actual process of pregnancy and birth, with all their physical challenges.

The role of wife and mother will always be a ministry in its own right for women and is not to be minimized or neglected. God will always make a way for a woman to obey him in the type and degree of ministry responsibilities she takes on, if she will submit them to him.

Many times a woman does not fully walk in a prophet's mantle until her children are old enough to need less attention. This was the case with me, although I continually read my Bible at every opportunity, no matter how brief, and kept a regular prayer time while the children slept. I did not arise into my gifting until my youngest child was twelve years old.

A woman faces the issue of managing emotions and moods to a greater degree than a man and must also work with physical weakness to a greater degree than a man, but God will give her the strength and the grace that is needed. The natural role of wife and mother is a prophetic picture of the ministry of love, wisdom, nurturing, and caring for God's people.

Women also carry equal spiritual authority with the man in the operation of their ministry gifts.

A woman is free to express her gifts and her personality in the way God created her. She may be strong and outspoken, or sweet and quiet, or any combination of those traits. God will use a woman who is submitted and obedient in scriptural ways to action his purposes in the earth to the same degree he will use a man for those purposes.

God is now bringing a balance to the role of women who have moved from total suppression to extremes of rebellion and independence and are now learning what it is to stand in true authority, which does not need to operate in false submission. False submission is an expression of religion where a woman loses touch with who she is.

False submission is defined by a loss of personal will and personal spiritual gift operation and an inability to have or express personal opinions. The woman becomes so immersed in the man's will alone that her identity becomes blurred or even nonexistent.

This dynamic can also operate from a woman to another woman or man, or a man to either gender outside of marriage. It is often called codependency and can also be called control.

Sometimes women struggle to find a balance and become a harsh, abrasive authority model that needs to disrespect the man. God wants his daughters to be balanced whole people who know how to stand with men and work with them to complete God's plans.

Prophecy for the end-time women

I saw an army of women like Joan of Arc wearing their armor and mounted on their horses, ready to go to war. They are unafraid and determined to defeat the spirit realm. They are no longer willing to settle for less than God's best. They are focused on the kingdom of God and will not be distracted from their purpose. Each soldier takes their appointed place, their swords are sharp, their armor is shiny. They are filled with zeal for the house of God.

They take their zeal into the marketplace; and whether they are shopping, paying bills, caring for their families, or having fun with their friends, the zeal for God's house and his purposes continues to burn within them and overflows into every area of their lives. They no longer separate church time from social time; it all runs together, and their lives are not in separate capsules but cohesive and all directed into God's purposes. God is calling the women to arise and shake off the dust of confusion and apathy, pain, distress, and inferiority and to start to walk in their destiny.

This army of women have their arms extended to God, to their families, and to each other. They encircle each other with love, understanding, loyalty, and friendship. They will not betray each other but will support and encourage and strengthen each other. Their unity will scare the enemy. He will see that he can no longer divide and conquer and will run in fear. His strategies will be totally exposed this year; he can no longer hide them because the spirit of God will blow away the coverings and totally expose every hidden work of darkness.

Bonds of inferiority and intimidation will fall off their lives, false submission and bondage to religious roles will be broken, old wounds caused by being suppressed and treated unjustly will be healed. These wounds have been hidden below the surface, but God is uncovering them, and there will be instant healings. As the army drinks from the pool of God's spirit, divine power and strength floods their bodies, sickness goes, and miracles occur. A new level of physical strength is imparted to their bodies. Marriages are strengthened and together the couples laugh for joy.

There will be a new unity between men and women. The men will feel strengthened and empowered by the women; they will walk in unity step by step and start to recognize and walk in their spiritual authority.

The men will rise into their role of leadership.

New people will be gathered to the army; generals trained and equipped and drawn by God. They will feel called to support the army and will stand through every circumstance because they will know their place.

Hell shakes and trembles with fear as this army starts to move and shake the region.

The army is being refined. The true soldiers, those who are called, have heard the trumpet blow. Some will come from other nations this year; some will come from places of obscurity.

There is a spiritual alert to the army of God; it is time for them to stand, take their positions, and start to march in rank. The season of inaction is over; it is a season of kingdom dominion, when the kingdom of God will take dominion and authority both in the secular world and in the spiritual world. Some of the army will refuse to stand; some will stand but refuse to get into the correct rank, and some will even start to march but be unable to keep up. There is a place in the army for everyone, but God is requiring action.

This church is being refined and sharpened; it will start to operate in a new warfare edge. This is being increased, and there is a "green beret" team, which will lead the new season, a group of spiritual commandos who are rising to a new level of authority.

Strongholds that have resisted the gospel in the region and the growth of the church will be broken this year. Strongholds will crumble; it will appear to be instant, but in fact these strongholds have been weakened by the continual assault over a period of time, and the final blow will utterly shatter them. It is like the dam wall in the movie *Dambusters*. The bombs were dropped and appeared to make no difference and then suddenly the wall broke.

There is a reversing of the spiritual dominion at this time. Where there has been domination by tradition and religious thinking, there will be a new spirit of freedom, which will shatter mind-sets. It has been established in the heavenlies, and you will see the manifestation of this in the coming weeks.

There will be a new shout of triumph and victory in the house; great joy will rise, and this spirit of joy is being poured out now on individuals and on the church. There will be meetings where the manifest presence of God will come down, and the whole congregation will sing a song of the spirit. There will be miracles during the service.

God is gathering an elite team of soldiers that needs to be very sharp, very cohesive and very focused, and who will specifically pinpoint areas that need prayer; and as they pray and praise, there will be a quick calling into spiritual order. That which is not of God cannot stand in this season; those who are not called cannot stay. I saw the ranks tighten, walking closely together; there is no space left for disunity.

I also saw a distribution of weapons and armor to those who answer the call to the new level. Those who answer the call to the new level will be eager to face all challenges and receive the new weapons and armor. Individual and specifically tailored armor will be given to each person.

They will not have to wear the armor of another person. It was like the picture of aid distribution after a disaster, where the people run and grab; they are so eager to have it.

The negative voice will be silenced by the spirit of God. The shout of joy and triumph will drown it out; it will be unable to be heard.

The first strategy of the enemy to stop the wall being built was criticism of the process and quality of the building (Nehemiah 4:3).

I believe this is what has been happening and is now being exposed and dealt with; those whose heart is not in the work will deposition themselves.

The second strategy was to fight and stir up trouble.

When they saw gaps being closed they became angry and tried to stir up trouble, but a guard was posted night and day to stop people sneaking in at night and destroying the work (verses 7, 8).

The third strategy was to weaken the laborers because there was so much rubble (criticism of leaders) they could not build.

Nehemiah countered this by guarding the weak points and encouraging the people not to be afraid of the enemy. They then were able to put their focus on building the wall because some were set to guard and some were set to build (verse 10).

They all worked with weapons in their hands, but the man who sounded the trumpet stayed by Nehemiah, and they never put down their weapons.

God's new Joel army will contain men, women, and children; it will also contain very old people who will be used mightily in the end times, all arm in arm and walking together, defeating disunity and personal agendas to activate the kingdom of God upon the earth.

God has called and raised up women with a special anointing as healers and restorers, to assist with the healing process of the relationships between men and women, individuals, and nations.

There will also be healing of families, restoration of prodigals, and continuing release of women who live in nations where they are suppressed. God will speak up for those women, and they will initiate an outpouring of the Holy Spirit in their nations.

Women who are gifted with the office of prophet (or prophetess, whichever you prefer) will also walk in all manifestations of the prophetic mantle, as God has called them.

Summary

The ability to adapt to change and flow with changing seasons and roles is an essential ingredient in the life of the prophetic person. Without flexibility and an open heart to receive the changes that God initiates, we will be stuck in the past and unable to progress.

The ability to recognize the current season in our lives releases us to walk into the next season

We don't need to understand every detail and aspect of the season, but we do need to be aware when God is changing our mantle or enlarging our mantle.

He changes our mantle by moving us totally out of one aspect of ministry into another. He enlarges our mantle by increasing the impact and effectiveness of our gift operation or leading us into a totally new manifestation of gifting.

Now is the time to allow God to soften us so that we can be flexible enough to move with what he is doing now.

PART II

THE BATTLE MANUAL FOR PROPHETIC WARRIORS

Chapter 1

Removing the Arrows and Shaping the Armor

During the journey from new Christian to prophetic warrior, there will be many occasions when the battle leaves wounds and scars.

The difference between a wound and a scar is that a wound is still painful and may be infected, creating a distraction; and a scar is healed and is evidence of a victory over the assignment of death and destruction.

It is necessary for wounded warriors to be healed so that their ministry is not contaminated and misdirected because of unhealed wounds. Arrows are words that have been spoken against us. They have the power to wound deeply and even to kill or destroy our ministry if they are not dealt with. Arrows must be removed for the wounds to heal, and this is done by

- forgiving those who have shot the arrows
- releasing those people from our judgments against them
- letting go of the offense—that is, not holding a grudge against them
- no longer blaming them for how we feel today or how our ministries have been affected

Words can be hurtful simply because of the content, more hurtful because of the closeness of our relationship with that person or devastating because they are empowered by a demonic spirit. This is why the word of God speaks so strongly of the need to take authority over the words we speak. God created everything by his words, and he has given us great authority to speak life or death over ourselves and others.

No one has the power to rob us of our ministry, but our own decisions and reactions may do so, if we do not quickly resolve our heart's attitudes.

Warriors need to keep their hearts positioned correctly, as when they allow their attitudes and actions to be controlled by wounding, they create holes in their spiritual armor that can allow enemy attack.

Some wounds occur directly through the spirit realm attacking us, and some occur because of the words and actions of people. Many soldiers are killed by friendly fire in wars, and certainly all of us, even Jesus, have been "wounded in the house of our friends."

The people we are close to, our spiritual authorities and those we fellowship with, have the most power to wound us because we have opened our hearts to them and so do not have defense mechanisms in place to stop those words or actions impacting our hearts.

Wounds from the spirit realm can be caused because we

- **engage in battles God has not called us to (1 Samuel 30:8, Acts 19:16)**

David returned from battle exhausted to find his family had been stolen, and he had to make a decision about tactics at a time when his own heart was in deep distress. He could have followed his natural instincts to rescue his family, but he had learned from his mistakes that he needed God to bless and endorse his battles. So he asked God for divine wisdom, and God released him to go with a promise of full recovery of all he had lost. The natural mind is at war with the spiritual mind; we have the mind of Christ, his wisdom, and his knowledge; and it is essential to draw on that mind of Christ and not use our own wisdom and knowledge even when it seems obvious to engage in a battle.

- **are not in a place of committed fellowship and accountable relationship with church leaders**

Lone rangers are vulnerable to the spirit realm, and the Bible clearly illustrates this, describing the threefold cord, which does not break. The more strands a rope has, the stronger it is, and we see the trinity modelling the power of the unity. Jesus spoke of his submission to the Father, only doing what his Father said, and this powerful principle is increasingly important as a warrior ascends into higher levels of spiritual warfare.

To complete your assignment, you will have to

- **let go of false accusation, intimidation, and criticism (1 Samuel 17:28-36).**
- **get your armor personally fitted.**

Paul talks about the "whole and complete" armor of God in Ephesians 6. All aspects of the armor need to be applied to our lives, however, as we all have strengths and weakness in certain areas. The Holy Spirit will "train our hands for war and our fingers for battle" by adjusting these areas of our lives so that they no longer are a place of vulnerability.

By allowing the Holy Spirit and our mentors and friends to speak to us of our weaknesses, we have increased protection, as we can become aware of vulnerable areas in our lives that we would not otherwise have seen.

The pressures and battles that come against us help to form our armor to fit us individually. David could not wear Saul's armor because he had not "tested" it. He had not used it in battle and proven that it worked. It was made for another person, not for him (1 Samuel 17: 34-39).

We all develop our revelation of truth, righteousness, faith, salvation, prayer, and the word, which are the key components of our armor, at different stages and seasons of our life. These components of the armor must be continually developed and strengthened to enable us to stand in victory and win the battles.

Our development of the armor determines the level of battle we can engage in and overcome.

Revelation of the word in all of these areas produces authority and confidence in the ability of the armor to protect us.

Revelation needs to be received on the battlefield, as revelation gives us authority to warfare in that area, and when we win that battle, we then have more authority in that area. What we receive by revelation, we then have authority in that area.

We put the armor on by faith, but we develop it through practice. By reason of use, our spiritual senses are exercised and strengthened (Hebrews 5:14).

David used the armor and weapons he had become competent in, the staff, the stones, his relationship with God and revelation of the power of God, and the strength of covenant; and in his sphere of authority, he defeated the enemy he had been assigned to by God.

That which you prove in your own field of battle becomes yours to possess and you are able to then take it into a new battlefield.

Shape your lifestyle to your calling

Identify your assignments, gifts, and calling. A sense of destiny and calling is within each of us, and this is confirmed by prophecy, input from leadership, personal revelation, and life experience and preferences.

It is vital to recognize spiritual gifts and passions and prayerfully undertake whatever training, both "on the job" and educational, that will fit your calling.

Some people are called exclusively to the marketplace, to business, or to secular employment; and these are valid areas of ministry into which we can take the gospel and Christian values. It is common to train for these areas through secular education, but it is important also to engage in training for spiritual warfare and know how to engage the enemy that would oppose your assignment. Spiritual wickedness in high places establishes thrones of iniquity in the marketplace. If you don't walk in authority over these wicked spirits, you will not complete the spiritual side of your assignment to the marketplace.

There will also be spiritual assignments within the local church that God will call us to; some people are called to minister in churches, but our everyday life also needs to impact our circle of influence. We all have "gatekeeper" roles in our family, workplace, and personal finance as well as our personal spiritual walk with God.

Church roles may involve practical service, prayer support, platform ministry, or leadership.

Paul says that no man who wars "entangles" himself with the affairs of this life; he was talking about the need for those who teach the word to be free to study and prepare and also for all who engage in spiritual warfare to give their main focus to the call of God and not be distracted by even those things that are good and necessary but to have our priorities in order.

To entangle means to entwine. **Imagine many ropes being left loose on the deck of a ship, which cause a person to trip because the ropes wrap themselves around their feet in such a way that it becomes impossible to move, and help is then needed to become free** (2 Timothy 2:4).

The concept is if you are entangled with something that is tripping you up and keeping you from what God has assigned you to do, you need to reevaluate what you are doing.

God says he will "train our hands for war and our fingers for battle." This is *his responsibility,* and he will send or allow those pressures that will shape us to fit our calling (Psalms 144:1).

Our responsibility is to

- walk in the spirit so that we do not fulfill the lusts of the flesh (Galatians 5:160).
- filter our activities, the things we look at, the things we hear so that our spirit is strengthened.
- study to show ourselves approved; build those areas of training that fit our gifts and calling (2 Timothy 2:14).
- stay positioned in the place and responsibilities he has called us to.

Chapter 2

The Forming of a Warrior

Every Christian needs to walk victoriously in areas of spiritual warfare. We do not seek warfare, but it seeks us. This is because the spirit realm is challenged because of who we are in Christ and who we have become in Christ.

By faith we are victorious overcomers, seated at the right hand of Christ, and given authority to bind and loose. Sometimes the enemy sees and accepts that more than we do.

We are in the process of becoming those victorious warriors, and God allows giants to come so that we ourselves can develop spiritual muscle by killing them.

God did not remove all the giants from the promised land at once. The people themselves destroyed (or did not destroy) those giants or tribes of people who opposed them.

We must fight to possess our promises and destroy all the works of the enemy that oppose those promises.

An essential part of this process is to overcome fear and intimidation and overcome generational bondages (Judges 6:11-16).

Gideon was a man called to be a judge and a prophet but also a man who face enormous giants of fear, intimidation, and inherited generational bondages. He had to walk the pathway that everyone must walk to enter into the personal wholeness that will give them the strength to carry their mantle.

Let's look at the life of Gideon and his process of growth. We see this process in Judges 6.

Step one: Gideon faced his identity issue

He said, "I am the weakest, and my father's house is the weakest." He spoke out loud the hidden springs of his heart and, perhaps for the first time, truly heard what he thought about himself. Identifying the source of our issue is an essential first step in the healing process (Judges 6:15).

Step two: partnered with God

He needed to accept that God was with him and draw on God's strength, disregarding his own weaknesses (Judges 6:16).

Step three: separated himself from his father's iniquities

He did this by obeying God when he was told to pull down the altar to Baal, which had been built by his father. His father worshipped at this altar, and Gideon needed to release himself from the effects of that idol worship. When he did so, he also released his father, as his father came to his defense and renounced Baal when confronted by the angry men about his son's actions. He learned a lesson in spiritual warfare as he overcame that spirit of Baal on his own behalf and his father's. We gain authority in the areas we have personally overcome. This was the first step in the development of his prophet's mantle (Judges 6:25, 26).

Giants that stand before us are specific to that which we are called to overcome, and that which we hate is often the very thing we are called to destroy.

Let us look at the life of David as a further example of overcoming fear and intimidation.

Step one: David had to deal with fear and intimidation (1 Samuel 17:28-33).

David had to deal with the fear of wild animals first and then with the fear and intimidation that came against him through his family and then that which came through the other soldiers, and finally he faced his first major giant—Goliath.

The fear of wild animals was a legitimate and natural fear but still one that he had to deal with as a prophetic type and shadow of establishing his authority over God's creation and also his authority over the giant he would have to kill to establish his mantle.

His family mocked him and accused him of false motives, challenging his presence and calling it a desire to see the battle instead of what it was, a response to his father's request.

The king quite legitimately questioned his youth and inexperience and the lack of a suit of armor, which would fit him. But David knew the source of his authority and power. He spoke of his God, who helped him to kill the lion and the bear and who would help him kill Goliath.

David recognized the cause, a giant who was not in covenant with God (uncircumcised), challenging God's people. He knew his position as a man in covenant with his God and knew that covenant was stronger than human strength.

He then went on to deal with fear at a whole new level in the palace as Saul set out to kill him, and he lived in constant danger of death even when he fled from the palace into the wilderness.

Step two: David had to learn to take responsibility that would come to a man called to be king.

He would have to take responsibility for the lives of others, and taking care of his sheep was a step on this pathway.

The lion and the bear David killed were symbolic of the predators that would come against God's people. They preyed upon the sheep, used intimidation and strength and stealth to kill the flock.

These represented the heathen nations, which preyed upon, killed, and enslaved Israel. David was called to be a deliverer of God's people, and this was expressed by his words in 1 Samuel 17: 35—"I delivered the lamb." David knew he was a deliverer, and he understood the role of a deliverer. Because of this, he acknowledged that the Lord had been his deliverer, and he was also called to deliver God's flock.

Step three: David had to kill that which opposed God and his people (Goliath).

As a man called to be prophet, he had to walk in his spiritual authority and lead others into that place as well. He could not allow his God to be mocked or God's people to be destroyed. His battle was now more about God's people than his limited area of responsibility for his father's flock. His sphere of authority increased because he had proved himself in the wilderness.

Step four: David had to kill his desire for self-justification and revenge and allow God to be his vindicator.

He had to keep his focus on his calling even when those in authority over him opposed it. He stayed in the palace until the threat against him was so great that God provided a way out through Jonathan, the son of King Saul. God will use the most surprising people to enable us to escape places of death and establish ourselves in destiny.

Step five: David had to walk in seasons of hiding without seeking promotion.

He was unknown in the wilderness and unknown by the prophet Samuel, but at the right time God called him out of that hidden place to the attention of prophets and kings.

He was unknown on the battlefield, but God made a place to reveal his gifts. His gifts made way for him and promoted him but did not release him to the throne at that time.

He was sent alone and unknown in the next wilderness after he left the palace, and again he was being processed to own the authority of a new level, to ascend the throne.

Step six: David had to endure hardness (2 Timothy 2:3).

Warriors need to be able to live in physical hardness or luxury. The apostle Paul talks about all the hardships of his life and how he endured them for the Gospel. He tells his spiritual son Timothy to endure hardness as a good soldier. David lived in deserts and in the luxury of a palace and kept his focus in both places. It is important not to be distracted by either comfort and luxury or hardship. The battle is the same against principalities and powers no matter what our current status.

Step seven: David had to live in caves (1 Samuel 22-24).

Cave dwelling is a necessary part of soldiering; David lived in caves called Adullam and Engedi. In Adullam he learned to lead problem people, distressed, discontented, and in debt; in Engedi he learned to honor authorities even when they were destructive to him and his calling. Both of these areas of warfare must be overcome consistently by those who would sit on thrones of authority.

Other prophets were hidden in caves to preserve their lives. There are season when God will hide us to keep us from those who would harm us or to allow us time to refresh and recover (1 Kings 18:4).

Step eight: David had to survive assignments of destruction (1 Samuel 18: 9, 11, 25).

The enemy desires to kill us but cannot do this while our lives are continually committed to and submitted to our God. Nevertheless, he will cause us as much discomfort as he can and try to take our energy and focus away from God's purposes.

Step nine: David had to survive promotion.

The wilderness and the battle bring tremendous challenges, but promotion also brings its own unique challenges. When he became king, David was given unlimited power, and those areas of his life that were still weak were now revealed. New levels of authority reveal our sin and weakness at a new level, and it is necessary for us to allow the Holy Spirit to cleanse, heal, and restore those things that are not complete in our lives. They may have been healed before, but God strips away the layers so that we can receive a new and deeper level of healing for each new season.

Chapter 3

Know Your Authority

Spiritual authority is delegated from Jesus to us; we carry the king's seal and letter of authority to act in his name. We are his ambassadors with all the authority of his kingdom and throne (Matthew 28:16).

"I give you power and authority over all the power of the enemy" (Luke 10:19).

Our delegated authority operates in three specific areas:

- Power to cure diseases (Luke 9:1)
- Power over the demonic (Luke 10:19)
- Power to make disciples (Matthew 28:18-20)

Spiritual authority is

- hierarchal.
- developed through practice.
- linked to spiritual gifts / governmental mantles.
- linked to assignment and spheres; you have authority over what God has told you to do or given you responsibility for.

Christ has defeated Satan and his army through the cross and the resurrection but has left his church as the occupation army to enforce his delegated authority in the earth until he returns. Just as there are hierarchies of demons and angels, so there is an authority hierarchy of spiritual mantles and spheres. If we operate outside of the mantle and sphere we have, then we become vulnerable to backlash from the enemy.

Adam had authority over the garden and the animals; he was given authority to name the animals, which established that authority. When he and Eve ate from the forbidden tree, they went outside of their permitted authority and therefore received the consequences of that in their own lives and the lives of their generations, until the cross and the resurrection.

We can rebuke any spirit that attacks what we are personally responsible for, our health, our family, our ministry.

We should not directly rebuke regional spirits unless we have a fivefold office and are in unity with other people of similar spiritual rank.

We can rebuke spirits on the lives of individuals as God leads us.

Spiritual warfare is not only about rebuking spirits but releasing praise and worship and praying the answer rather than laboring to release and overcome the problem. It is also about living in the opposite spirit and declaring the answer over our own lives and the lives of others. We can do this safely after having repented of any of our sin, forgiven others, and received our healing from God, which removes the dwelling place for any demonic activity and should be the first response to demonic oppression.

The enemy will have no landing place in us and will automatically cease operations. He may come back from time to time to test the waters and see if the person will allow him any access, but his authority is limited to what he is given permission to do by individuals.

Legally/positional, we have been given the authority and power of attorney to rule over the demonic realm, but as in a natural army, like rank addresses like rank. Privates do not rebuke generals but deploy under their authority, carrying out their battle plans.

Individuals with governmental office mantles have a greater level of authority and so are able to address spiritual situations, which have the involvement, or regional or national spirits. Even so, there is strength and safety in numbers, and teams will be more successful in this area than solitary people (Ephesians 4).

Identifying spiritual authority levels
Both your understanding of your spiritual authority and your spiritual mantle needs to be equal to what you address in the spirit.
These scriptures list the ranks of demonic powers:
Ephesians 3:10, 6:12; Colossians 1:16, 2:15; Romans 8:38; Ephesians 6:12; Colossians 2:15
They are identified as the following:

- Principalities
- Powers
- Rulers of the darkness of the world
- Spiritual wickedness in high places
- Thrones and dominions

Prayer strategy for addressing the demonic

Types of Spirits and Prayer Strategies
Territorial spirits
National

Prayer strategy: National pastors get together in unity and pray
Regional
Prayer strategy: Regional pastors get together in unity and pray
Specific task spirits
Sow confusion, division, and harass and hinder individuals and churches.
Prayer strategy: Individuals / prayer teams
Generational spirits
Inherited/activated through open doorways of sin
Prayer strategy: Individuals/fathers/pastors/counselors

Legal/Positional Authority

We have received legal or positional authority; however, that authority must be developed to become activated and effective in our lives

"I give you power and authority over all the power of the enemy" (Luke 10:19).

The spiritual authority (dominion) that was lost in the Garden of Eden was taken back by Jesus through the cross and the resurrection. *Power of attorney* has now been given to us to enforce his authority upon the earth until he comes back (Matthew 28:18; Luke 9:1, 13).

There are two dimensions to this power of attorney:

- **Authority, which equals superhuman jurisdiction, as in *Strong's Concordance* definition.**
  1849. *exousia, ex-oo-see'-ah;* from G1832 (in the sense of ability); privilege, i.e., (subj.) force, capacity, competency, freedom, or (obj.) mastery (concr. magistrate, superhuman, potentate, token of control),

delegated influence: authority, jurisdiction, liberty, power, right, strength.

This authority gives the power to rule over circumstances, including weather and demonic forces through the spoken word. We see this illustrated when Jesus silenced the storm on Galilee. The disciples comment was, "Even the winds and waves obey him." His authority was also recognized as he taught them, producing comments like, "We never heard anyone teach with such authority."

His authority was recognized automatically by the demonic realm before he spoke. They screamed out of people, begged to be sent into pigs rather than be without a physical body. They did not argue with Jesus's right to cast them out and knew they needed his permission to even enter the pigs. Pigs were unclean animals under Jewish law, and no doubt the demons felt comfortable in an unclean animal since they were not allowed to stay in the favorite host, humanity.

By possessing a human made in God's image, they were mocking God and trying to gain the authority that God intended man to have.

- **Power which equals strength**
  1411. dunamis, doo'-nam-is; from G1410; force (lit. or fig.); spec. miraculous power (usually by impl. a miracle itself):—ability, abundance, meaning, might (-ily, -y, -y deed), (worker of) miracle (-s), power, strength, violence, mighty (wonderful) (*Strong's Concordance*)

We get the word dynamite from the Greek word *dunamis*, and it expresses the power to create chaos. The enemy can create confusion and chaos but does not have jurisdiction or *exousia* as redeemed mankind does.

Our spiritual authority is activated and developed through the following:

1. The keys Jesus has given us (Matthew 16:19)

We bind and we lose in heaven and in earth through faith-filled prophetic declaration which has been delegated to us by Jesus. (Matthew 28:18-20)

2. The weapons of our warfare (2 Corinthians 10:4-6)

These weapons are not those of our flesh but those which God has given us. We must use spiritual weapons to fight spiritual battles. Fleshly ways do not destroy spiritual strongholds.

The blood of the lamb	(Revelation 12:11)
The words of our mouth	(Proverbs 18:21)
The name of Jesus	(John 14:14, Romans 14:11, Philippians 2:10)
The word of God	(Hebrews 4:12)
The armor of God	(Ephesians 6:10)
Renewing the mind	(2 Corinthians 10:5)
Praise and worship	(Acts 16:24)

We are now responsible for binding and releasing demonic forces and enforcing God's will through the words of our mouth in prayer and declaration.

We have received legal or positional authority; however, that authority must be developed to become activated and effective in our lives.

3. **Correct positioning**

Spiritually:

- We are seated in heavenly places (Ephesians 1:3).
- We are joint heirs with Christ (Romans 8:17).
- We are operating in our gifts (1 Corinthians 12).
- We are training for our calling (2 Timothy 2:15).
- We are separated to win the battle (2 Timothy 2:3, 4).

Geographically:

Positioned strategically at our battle stations for this season (Esther 2:12-17, 4:14).

Before the crucifixion, when mankind had no delegated authority, we see that a Jewish woman called Esther saved her people through submission and obedience to God. God breathed on and anointed her submission and obedience. How much more can we do with the indwelling Holy Spirit in our lives.

Let's look at the life of Esther

Vashti, the previous queen, disobeyed the king and dishonored his authority, and this caused her to lose her position. This caused the king to look for another queen who would respect him. Esther was prepared through the favor she received in her hidden season.

She was positioned and prepared when her opportunity came.

She had a wise heart, which could discern the times and seasons; she was called to intercede for her nation for *such a time as this* (Esther 4:14).

She had a courageous heart and was willing to risk death, she said, "If I perish, I perish".(Esther 4:16)

She was then given *favor* to speak to the king, which represents the power to speak to the ruling heathen spirit realm of the day.

She was given *favor* to ask for half the kingdom; she could have whatever she wanted within those limits.

Favor is released through our positioning and obedience, which then enables us to

- expose evil (Esther 7:1-5).
- reverse the plans of the enemy (Haman killed on gallows intended for Mordecai) (Esther 7:7-10).
- release new levels of authority (Esther 8:1-4).
- change circumstances, spirit realms, and laws (only the king could revoke the law, but Esther changed it) (Esther 8:5-8).
- destroy our enemies and restore what is stolen (Esther 8:11-13).
- plunder the enemie's goods
- activate deliverance and freedom for God's people
- release the city and make it rejoice, release God's people

When evil ruled, the city was perplexed (Esther 3:15).

When the power of evil was overthrown, the city of Shushan rejoiced and was glad; and God's people had light, gladness, joy, and honor (Esther 8:15, 16).

- destroy ungodly seed so that our enemy cannot rise again or build up secret power.

Haman's sons were hanged (Esther 9:13).

- free our nation (Esther 9:29). Gives influence in governments; she was given authority to write new laws because she went to the throne room and touched the scepter (Esther 10:3).

Summary

Esther fasted, changed her garments (mantle), and went to the throne room (prayer).

She demonstrated the three levels of authority we need to develop so that we can fully embrace the call of God. She was positioned and prepared as a concubine in the king's palace. This was such an unlikely place to find destiny, but God uses unlikely places, people, and circumstances to position us for his purposes.

In that place she found favor and had authority for her own needs because of that favor. She was given anything she asked for to prepare to meet the king. Esther was called before the king and heard through Mordecai of a plan to destroy her people.

She had to make a significant choice to stay in a place where her own needs were met and ignore the needs of her people or to take a huge risk and walk into a new level of authority. She chose to take that risk, and because she let go of her own safety, she now walked into a place of authority where she had the power to meet the needs of others.

Eventually, she walked into third-level authority, which was governmental. She not only saved the nation but she also was given authority to write new laws. This was unheard of at that time, and it all happened because she walked in obedience, wisdom, and faith.

We see throughout scripture that deliverers arose to save the nation of Israel every time they had fallen into idol worship or captivity because of their sin. God is determined to cause his promises to his people to be fulfilled.

For example:

Joseph was positioned in both prison and palace and activated deliverance from both (Genesis 50:20).
Four lepers saved their city (2 Kings 7:3).
Many other deliverers, including Deborah, Samson, Joshua, and all the prophets like Elijah, Elisha, Jeremiah, Paul, Peter, and thousands of modern-day heroes and heroines, continue to bring freedom and activate God's purposes.

Walking in authority in prayer means we

- prepare our hearts.
- obey God and authorities—unless the authorities ask us to disobey God's word.
- position ourselves in the throne room and touch the scepter.
- use wisdom and discernment.
- receive the favor to activate the authority.
- are submitted to the lordship of Christ (Matthew 8:9, Luke 7:8).
- are submitted to local church authority (Hebrews 13:17-18).
- have healthy relationships (Matthew18:34, 35; 5:24).
- are submitted in marriage (Ephesians 5:22, 1 Peter 3:7).
- are able to work under delegated authority (Matthew 8:9).

21st Century Prophet

To enlarge our authority it is essential to learn to hear and obey God's voice so that we can receive intelligence reports of the enemies' plans. Our spiritual discernment needs to be constantly activated so that we stay alert and up to date with the season we are in (Hebrews 5:14).

CHAPTER 4

Know Your Enemy

Wherever there is consistent sin in the lives of an individual, a place is made for demonic spirits to oppress the soul of that person.

Any manifestation of the carnal man can make place for a spirit to occupy a place in an individual life or collectively in the life of a church.

Their only operating place resides around individuals; and the principle of putting to death the works of the flesh, repentance, forgiveness, and emotional healing releases us from the power of these spirits and binds their operations in the local church. A Christian cannot be possessed by an evil spirit, as the Holy Spirit lives in them and darkness and light cannot live together, but places of oppression and strongholds give influence to evil spirits.

When any sin becomes entrenched in the life of individuals or a church, it has the potential to become national sin, with the majority of the people in the nation being affected by it. Everyone will not necessarily become involved in that sin, but they will feel the oppression and perhaps temptation of it.

A place is then made for high-level demonic spirits to take ownership of a geographical region because the people to whom God gave authority over the earth have surrendered that authority to the enemy.

A wise warrior recognizes and evaluates his enemy; he does not fear them or glorify them, but neither does he ignore them. Preparation and alertness are essential attributes of warriors. The Bible tells us to stay alert as our enemy looks for opportunities. He is legally defeated at the cross but is an opportunist and will take any opportunities left open to him by the carelessness or sin of his target (1 Peter 5:8).

The Bible shows us the hierarchy of angels and demons and likens our spiritual war to an army in which like rank deals directly with each other. It is important to know our enemy and know our sphere of authority as discussed in the previous chapter.

I am not discussing the rankings of demons and angels in detail, as there are many excellent publications that have already done this. This is just an overview to put the battle in context.

These scriptures list the ranks of demonic powers:

Ephesians 3:10, 6:12; Colossians 1:16, 2:15; Romans 8:38

They are called principalities, powers, and rulers of the darkness of this world, spiritual wickedness in high places, thrones, and dominions.

Old Testament thrones of iniquity that were established by individual sin:

(Iniquity is sin that is sown into generations and goes down the family line or becomes established in regions or nations.)

For instance

The Iniquity of rebellion: Adam and Eve defiled mankind (Genesis 11-3)

The Iniquity of murder and sibling rivalry established: Cain killed Abel (Genesis 4:8)

We need to identify what is opposing us. Is it man, our own fleshly desires, or demonic forces? The scriptures say that we should submit to God and resist the enemy, and a good prayer to pray is "Father, if this is from you, I submit to it. If it is from the enemy, I bind it and resist it in Jesus's name." If it is our own un-regenerated thoughts or desires, we need to put them to death ourselves, pulling down strongholds that disagree with God's word and crucifying our self-will (James 4:7, Ephesians 4:27).

- We need to know our enemy.
- We need to know our calling and position in the battle.
- We need to know our current assignments.
- Doorways or areas of permission for the demonic to attack need to be closed.
- Our own lives need to be submitted to God and cleansed.

Chapter 5

Gremlins in the Church

The church—that living, breathing entity composed of people who are at various stages of spiritual development, is in a state of growth and maturity, which changes constantly. The corporate authority of that church is very powerful when the people are unified and on the alert to watch what God is doing now. It is the most powerful entity on planet earth but is not yet walking in that power. Wherever the church that exalts Jesus Christ and his word is progressing, the enemy will increase his attempts to divide and conquer. His only tactics are lies, lies, and more lies, confusion, distraction, and division; but he will use them to great effect if God's people allow him to.

We see certain manifestations, which occurred amongst the tribes of Israel from the time they began their journey out of Egypt. While they were in Egypt, the attack against them was to destroy and annihilate them through slavery. God allowed this because of their constant sin, but when they finally cried out to him in desperation, God responded to them and sent Moses to intercede with Pharaoh for them.

As they moved forward to their promised land, certain ruling spirits arose against them and from among them.

1. The spirit of Pharaoh.

This was the spirit that kept them enslaved in Egypt but which they also carried with them as they travelled through the wilderness. It manifested as dissatisfaction with their food and conditions and especially with their desire to create their own gods, as they had come under that spirit realm in Egypt. They looked back to what their souls had liked about Egypt and forgot about the slavery conditions, and they created their own golden calf to worship using the gold God had given them that had been the property of their enemies.

In the church today, this spirit manifests as the following:
Spiritual abuse of gifts by leaders (Exodus 1, 2)

The spirit of Pharaoh kept Israel from its destiny by enslaving the mind and will of the people for the purpose of using their labor to build the kingdom of Pharaoh. This can occur when a church leader wants to use the gifts and labor of the people for their own personal agenda and is unwilling to allow people to grow and develop in their own gifts, which would then allow them to leave a position or role in the church and grow into their own ministry. This should not be confused with the true care of a shepherd, who does not want to allow that person to move into something bigger before they are mature enough to handle it. When this spirit is operating, it rules with harshness and severity, as described in Exodus, and has no care or concern for the health, happiness, or personal fulfillment of the person. Cruelty is the normal standard for this spirit when it operates in its fullness.

It uses cruel and harsh words to control, requires a task to be completed without regard to the working conditions or equipment available, and harshly judges the results. There is usually no praise or encouragement, just criticism, which will keep the spirit of that person suppressed and without the motivation to be proactive or inspirational.

It suppresses fruitfulness by not allowing a person to improvise or be creative and limits what kind of fruit can be grown. For instance, it will occupy people with menial tasks, not allowing them to function in their strongest gift.

It does this for the purpose of keeping people from their destiny so that they will not lose their usefulness to the leader. It kills vision and reproduction except on its own terms. People operating in a situation where this spirit operates are very discouraged, unreasonably tired, and lacking enthusiasm.

2. The spirit of Korah (Numbers 16)

This spirit brings a leadership challenge to the senior leader from other leaders serving under their authority.

It does this through open confrontation and false accusation, which challenges the leader's style. It sometimes compares them to a leader who has left, especially one whom the people loved and respected. It likes to start grievances against the leaders and often does this by collecting people into a small group, usually in a home, and speaking against their leader.

This creates an atmosphere of intimacy and a sense of being in the confidence of that leader who is operating under that spirit. We see that Miriam and Aaron talked in the tent and contaminated others before they confronted Moses. It will sometimes claim the anointing has left the leader, saying things like, "Well, he or she used to be anointed but . . ." Either way, it sows doubt about the suitability and calling of the senior leader. It will also promote itself, through that person, as the next leader saying they will change those things that the people don't like.

It promotes a level playing field culture, saying "we are as good as them" but ignoring the call of God on the life of the senior leader who has been placed there by God.

3. The spirit of Absalom (2 Samuel 15)

This is a leadership challenge by family and friends against a leader that operates through deception and stealth. Like the spirit of Korah, it will start by criticizing the leader but, in this case, makes them out to be uncaring about the people's welfare. This person who is challenging their leader will steal authority that is not theirs, positioning themselves into a place where the people go to them first, even though this has not been authorized.

Their motive is not to relieve the senior leader's workload but to steal the hearts of the people. It is a form of spiritual adultery only in church leadership instead of between a couple. It is usually birthed in offense. We see that Absalom felt unheard and overlooked by his father, David, and so he sowed discord and contempt and offense to the people. It is very subtle, emphasizing its own ability to help rather than the defects of the leader. It operates schemes, setting others up to take the blame and hiding its own involvement.

Ultimately it can dethrone the king because by the time the disloyalty is seen the people's confidence in that leader is weakened and divided.

4. The spirit of Jezebel (1 Kings 16-18, 1 Kings 30:31, 33)

This operates as an open power grab or as hidden destruction. It attacks leaders and prophets, but especially prophets, including intercessors and those who may not be prophets but who carry a strong prophetic gift. It is threatened by the discernment of the prophet, as the prophet sees through the covering it wears before anyone else does. A person operating under this spirit is usually someone who has been very rejected and damaged and who seeks the power. They have become vulnerable because of their wounding, and so the spirit targets them. It is often, but not exclusively, a woman who is vulnerable to this spirit, usually because men have hurt her; so there is a doorway in her life that desires to bring down any man in authority.

This spirit

- allies itself with wickedness. Jezebel married Ahab, who is called the most wicked king who ever lived (1 Kings 16:30-33, 1 Kings 18, 19).
- tries to kill the true prophets.
- falsely accuses, making the innocent feel and look guilty.
- viciously retaliates, causing deep discouragement.
- tries to enthrone false prophets.
- creates loss of perspective.
- depositions from true position and purpose.
- breaks down the worship of the true God.
- stifles or substitutes the power of God.

There are many levels of the operation of this spirit from immature to fully mature, and great discernment and wisdom is needed to set a person free from its influence. The mature spirit is not often seen, and a person is not a "Jezebel" just because it has some influence over them.

5. The Pharisee spirit (Matthew 3)

This is a spirit of religion and often looks like it is engaging in true worship, but it is full of man's rules and restrictions.

Jesus confronted this spirit every time he encountered it by challenging the Pharisees, exposing their wrong beliefs and rebuking them for keeping others from true experiences with their God.

The Pharisees

- replaced God's word with their own rules.
- refused to accept change and were very inflexible.
- were spiritually blind, being unable to recognize their Messiah.
- were self-righteous and proud, basing their righteousness upon their own performance.
- prevented others from finding life.

Religion stifles the freedom of the Holy Spirit and keeps people trapped in a performance cycle as they strive to do everything they can to please God with their own works. It keeps the focus on obeying minor and unimportant man-made rules instead of finding God's ways. We obey God out of a heart that has been set free by his love, not because we depend upon our own goodness to please him. Cain's works were rejected because he bought his own works; and out of this a spirit of murder was released.

Religious people will criticize any changes made, no matter how necessary; they like to keep everything the same, including the furnishings of the church building. They like old songs and old-style music, regardless of whether they are still anointed or not. They will major on minor issues, like clothing style, and pick holes in the preacher's message, finding every mistake, no matter how minor.

6. The spirit of Saul (1 Samuel 10-18)

From senior leaders against gifted people because of jealousy and insecurity

This spirit attacks gifted leaders because of its own insecurity; it causes the suppression and death of leaders. It is similar to the spirit of Pharaoh in some ways but drives the leader out rather than confine them in the house of God for their own purposes.

This spirit

- controls through anger and intimidation (1 Samuel 15-18).
- refuses to give up position, even when the anointing is gone.
- drives out any leader or person it feels threatened by.
- uses leaders for their own purposes while allowing them to remain on the throne, not operate in their kingship gift. David was allowed to worship because it relieved the king's distress.

Saul was anointed as king, but God quickly regretted making him king (1 Samuel 15:11, 18:17).

Saul continued on the throne even though the anointing had left him, so because of his pride and rebellion, he opened a door for demonic spirits to operate through him. These spirits attacked the true anointed king, David. This spirit knows there is another king in waiting but may not be sure who it is so will attack anyone who looks like a candidate for its position. If the king in waiting is recognized by the spirit, the fury against that person will be especially strong, and the anger, which is attached to the spirit and the person yielding to it, will try to murder the gift or character of their successor.

7. The spirit of Python (Acts 16:16-19)

This spirit is named after a Greek god of the same name. This serpent was said to live in a cave where priestesses operated as diviners giving satanic messages to those who came to seek guidance.

Python stifles anointing and brings death in the church through the use of divination and false spiritual gifts or the absence of spiritual gifts. It causes a slow death, just like a true python who takes a long time to suffocate and then eat their prey.

- Suffocates the life of the spirit in a church or person
- Replaces the true gifts with false or kills the gifts
- Creates apathy and crushes hopes and dreams

People start to feel helpless and hopeless, like their dreams will never be fulfilled, so they give up and just go through the motions, waiting for death.

(See the warnings against divination and false prophecy [Deuteronomy 18:10, 11:18-14])

All of these spirit manifestations reflect the enemy's basic desire for worship, position, and power described in Isaiah 14.

Within the domain of each of these ruling spirits is idolatry, immorality, destruction of women and children, reversal of male female roles, and dethroning of rightful authority by various means. Some of their functions cross over, but usually there will be a domination of one spirit, which will challenge a church as we see in Revelation 3.

God named the strengths and weaknesses of each church, telling them what they needed to overcome to fulfill their calling as a church.

We are called to overcome, and when the workings of any of these spirits are revealed, then we can overcome them by declaring the opposite of what that spirit is trying to do in the church. We release the answer and take away any ground it has to operate by repenting and fasting, if necessary. No demonic spirit can stay or rule in an atmosphere that is clean. As each individual, especially the leaders, clean their personal house, then God's house will be clean. Repentance must begin in the house of God; he will cleanse the temple so that his house and the earth can be filled with his glory.

Chapter 6

Identify Your Battleground

Three types of Battle

1. **Overwhelmed and unable to determine strategy (2 Chronicles 20:1-30)**

That time when fear overwhelms you and you don't know where to turn. When surrounded by the enemy and without enough resources to win the battle, Jehoshaphat cried out, "We don't know what to do but our eyes are upon you."

Jehoshaphat reminded God of his power and the ways in which he had intervened for his people at other times. God had not forgotten, but Jehoshaphat was declaring the answer to the demonic spirit realm. In times of battle, when the odds look overwhelming, when everything seems impossible, use your voice to declare God's greatness, and this will release the answer. Place your life in God's hands.

The spirit of the Lord came upon Jahaziel, who prophesied that the battle was not theirs but God's.

Because Jehoshaphat cried out, God gave him instructions. Sometimes we fight and sometimes we stand still and let God fight for us.

Israel responded by standing before the Lord. They listened to the prophet, worshipped God, and then won the victory, taking more spoil than they could carry and having peace in their land. As they obeyed and listened to God's prophet, they found life.

2. Given strategy which you don't understand but must obey blindly (Joshua 5:1-9)

Separation from the past is essential to walk into a new season. God commanded Joshua to circumcise the whole generation who had been born in the wilderness and so had not been through this rite. Circumcision was the sign of the covenant made between God and his people, releasing everything God had to them and demonstrating his commitment to them.

After this important ceremony, Joshua received instructions from an angel of high authority to take the city of Jericho from the enemy. He was given a set of strange instructions, which would have made no sense at all to him, but because he was a seasoned warrior, he understood the value of unquestioning obedience to God.

God's instructions may seem foolish because he wants us to trust him and walk by faith, but when they are obeyed, they bring the answer we need.

Principles for victory from Joshua 6

Take the ark with you when you go into battle; take the manifest presence of God and the prophetic trumpet.

Sow prayer into the battle before you go, and the presence of God around your life will cause your enemy to fear because of your reputation as a warrior and one whom God defends.

Don't speak until God says to, and then say *only what he tells you* to and nothing else. Don't take what is accursed and what God says should be destroyed. Only take those objects that are made of metal, which can be purified by fire.

Deal with sin quickly. It will provide a landing place for the enemy to attack you if it is resident in your life. The Bible tells the story of a king who was killed on the battlefield by an arrow shot at random, which found a chink in his armor.

Go on in victory to the next battle; don't get stuck on the glories of the last battle but move on (Joshua 8).

3. Cause motivated, the cause is clear, but should I fight or leave it with God? (1 Samuel 30:8)

Your cause is clear and just, but don't presume you should automatically take action just because it is just. Don't fight battles God has not told you to fight even when it seems right to your natural understanding, because backlash can come from the enemy just as it came against David and Israel after they failed to consult God about going to Ai. They could not stand before their enemies because Achan had taken of the "accursed thing," and they went to battle presuming that they would be victorious because they had been in the past.

Always establish the leading of God before you become involved in a battle, and always make sure there is no sin in the camp.

The army marches on: communication, supply, and discipline

- **Communication**
  To communicate means to make someone a partaker of; it involves listening and speaking

The enemy works to cut off or confuse communication for us, because when he does so, the army defeats itself. Confusion, twisting of words, and misunderstanding, or even failure of the message to reach the intended person, stops the army in its tracks. When words are being twisted and there is a lot of misunderstanding, bind the blocking spirit and the twisting spirit; these are assigned to create confusion amongst the warriors.

The Internet and e-mail, and not to mention mobile phones, are a sign of the increasing need to communicate in a world, which is getting smaller and smaller. We see that when these services crash for any reason, our lives become halted because we have learned to depend upon them.

Failure to hear from God and failure to feed on his word will halt our forward progress, especially battle.

Failure to communicate clearly with the important people in our lives causes relationships to break down and go into confusion, which breaks down unity and destroys our effectiveness.

Communicate *to God*

Jehoshaphat said, "We don't know what to do, but our eyes are upon you." He then listened to the instructions from God and obeyed them (2 Chronicles).

Joshua listened to the Lord's instructions and obeyed them (Joshua 6:2).

David said, "Shall I go?" He listened for the answer and obeyed it (1 Samuel 30:8).

Communicate *to people*—to those we are responsible for or whom we lead.

To communicate is to make someone a partaker of what you are thinking and doing.

- **Supply**—the presence of God and of everything needed to go into battle (1 Samuel 4:3, 30:24).

The enemy steals our joy, our finances, and whatever else he can take hold of; but God supplies abundantly for our needs and even gives the spoil of battle to those who are support people; just because your only role in frontline ministry is to give financially or pray for those at the battlefront, it does not diminish the importance of your role. God recognizes this and lets the support team be partakers of the same blessing as those who lead the battle (1 Samuel 30:24).

Our financial needs depend upon the supply lines from God and others being open. If there is a blockage in the supply for your needs, ask God to show you what it is, and then use the weapons of your warfare to unblock it. A spirit of harassment will often attach and confuse supply lines; bind it in Jesus's name and provision will come.

God sends supplies to us through people, in unexpected ways and through unexpected sources. Don't limit him to the obvious.

Supply comes as a result of
request   (prayer)
giving   (to God and others)
communicating   (sharing needs, connecting with those in need)

There is a time to speak of your needs and a time to keep them private. Do as God leads you, and there will always be supply.

- **Discipline—doing battle how and when God tells you to**

Joshua followed the plan exactly; Moses followed the pattern for the tabernacle given to him by God down to the last detail.

Soldiers are trained to obey without understanding the reason; they are trained to endure hardship and to be courageous.

God is raising up his end-time army

- The army makes a clear sound to go into battle.
- The army waits on God.
- The army worships; Judah, the tribe of worshippers went first into battle.
- The army prevails.
- The army retrieves its own goods and plunders the spoil of the enemy.
- The army cares for its wounded.
- Clear communication, constant supply, and continual discipline produces a united and capable army.

"Endure suffering along with me, as a good soldier of Christ Jesus. [4]And as Christ's soldier, do not let yourself become tied up in the affairs of this life, for then you cannot satisfy the one who has enlisted you in his army. [5]Follow the Lord's rules for doing his work, just as an athlete either follows the rules or is disqualified and wins no prize. [6]Hardworking farmers are the first to enjoy the fruit of their labor. [7]Think about what I am saying. The Lord will give you understanding in all these things" (1 Timothy 2:3-7, New Living).

CHAPTER 7

Manifestations of Intercession

Intercession means:
Stand in the gap (stay and pray and take the hits), plead with God (engage in active discussion), occupy the territory (be there as an example), activate warfare.

Stand in the gap and just be there (Luke 19:13)

We are the occupation army; our role is to hold the territory till Jesus comes.

There is a time to advance, a time to step back and regroup, and a time just to stand and be immoveable. To effectively stand in the gap as a watchman, we must be awake and spiritually alert.

God wondered that there was no man to stand in the gap; he was surprised that the watchmen had lay down and gone to sleep (Isaiah 63:5, 59:15).

We see the same picture in the New Testament, people who have let their oil run out or gone to sleep so the thief can come in.

Watchmen should stay at their post until they are released by God; the watchman must be awake and at their post because if the thief knows the watchman is awake and positioned, then he will stay away. It is not always necessary to pray; sometimes just our presence binds the enemy. Sometimes God will say, "Just go and be there." Sometimes he will give a spirit of prayer to intercede for the situation.

Sometimes God will wake you up in the night. You may not know what to pray, so you can just pray in the spirit or perhaps just be awake and alert so you are available to go to prayer quickly if needed.

Noah is a great example of standing in the gap. He was told to build an ark and given the blueprints. It looked so ridiculous to build a giant boat in a region where there was no ocean, and the difficulty of getting that giant boat to the nearest ocean would have made it impossible to achieve. But he just stood and kept building because God had given him assignment and not released him from it. His name means "he will save us," and that ark was a type of salvation through entering the ark of Christ (Genesis 5:29).

He was five hundred years old before his destiny was fully activated, and without his persistence, all of mankind would have been wiped out. God looks for those who will stay at their post; we never fully know the impact of what we are doing until it is completed.

Keep praying, keep building, keep speaking; God is using you to keep the spirit realm open in your place of assignment.

Plead with God for the unsaved

Individuals. The story of the Good Samaritan is a prophetic picture of how our prayers for individual salvation are answered. Jesus himself finds the lost person; he sometimes does this in a power encounter with them and sometimes sends a friend to help them. He lifts them up, washes and heals their wounds, places them in a safe environment, and assigns someone to care for them as they recover (Luke 10:33).

Regions. Abraham prayed for the cities of Sodom and Gomorrah. He persisted and pleaded for mercy. Intercessors should always plead for mercy for sin. Abraham repeatedly falls on his face to intercede for those who sinned; Moses would also fall on his face to plead for mercy and to stay God's hand of judgment (Genesis 18).

God will appoint intercessors to pray for particular regions, and it is essential that they are linked to prophetic and apostolic leaders so that they do not come against regional spirits on their own. Prayer needs to come from heaven, from a position of authority; it is not the petition prayer but the prayer of authority that declares the answer that will meet regional needs.

Cities and regions become defiled by (the word "defile" means "to foul, pollute, contaminate")

- shedding of innocent blood (Numbers 35:33, Hosea 4:3, Genesis 4:10).
- sexual sin (Jeremiah 3:9).
- idolatry (Jeremiah 2:7, 3:2).

Lot had the responsibility to influence his city but did not pray for it and had to be rescued by Abraham.

Plead with God for his people

Moses was called to go before Pharaoh and speak directly to him, thus addressing the regional spirit. God sent him back to the palace he was raised in. God gave him access to that palace because he had been raised there; they knew him and therefore would listen to him.

God had given him an open door because of his orphan status. His intercession went from a command to Pharaoh to a power challenge with the local sorcerers, which then called down the plagues. Each plague represented a challenge to the ruling gods of Egypt. As each ruling throne of iniquity was overthrown, the chains that bound God's people to Egypt loosened.

God had heard the cry of his people, a cry of grief and bondage. God came down to see what was happening. Of course he knew, but he came down to see with an intention to act (Exodus 2:23).

Moses interceded only for the people of God, not for the nation of Egypt, as that was not his assignment.

In Exodus 44, we see that Moses reminded God that these were his people. God knew this, but Moses was positioning his plea for God's mercy on the basis of their relationship with God.

Israel did not pray for the city. The prayers of 4 million people could probably have changed the city. They were too defeated under that spirit of Pharaoh to see the need of their city.

Plead with God for your city

"Pray for the peace and welfare of the city to which I have caused you to be carried away captive, and pray to the Lord for it, for in the welfare of the city in which you live, you will have welfare" (Jeremiah 29:7).

The nation of Israel was taken captive to Babylon because of the rebellion against God, and in their captivity, they were unwilling to worship God. They said, "How can we sing the Lord's song in a strange land?" when their captors asked them to sing (Psalms 137:2)

But God raised up someone to stand in the gap for them. Nehemiah, who was also a captive, received the burden of the

Lord for the city of Jerusalem. They city had to be restored so that the promise of God to his people to dwell in their own land again could be fulfilled (Nehemiah 1).

Nehemiah heard a cry of grief and reproach and desolation, which arose from God's people, and responded with both prayer and action by asking the king to release him from his role and by going to the city. Prayer for a city is more effective when it is made in that city. Ezekiel was told to *stand in the city gates* and proclaim the word of the Lord.

God took his people back to Jerusalem after seventy years because of Nehemiah and Ezra. It took prayer *and* action to rebuild the city. God had asked them to pray for the city they were held captive in; perhaps Babylon would have turned to the true God if his people had prayed for it and not laid their harps of worship and prayer on a willow tree, mourning for what they had lost.

Nehemiah changed the sound of Jerusalem through enabling repentance, prayer, occupation, and action.

Sodom and Gomorrah, Egypt, and Babylon stayed bound by sin and idolatry; if God's people, who were resident in those cities, had interceded for them, perhaps they would have turned to the true God

We are city influencers. Jesus's disciples were told to keep watch but came under the oppression of the spirit realm and slept instead of praying. The Jews came under oppression of their city and did not want to sing or pray.

It is our mandate to change the sound of our city; each city has a sound, which can be changed through prayer, fasting, worship, and declaration. The sound of prayer should dominate every other sound so that both the shriek of sin and the cry of grief and reproach should be drowned out by the sounds of prayer dominating the atmosphere.

How to change the sound of your city

(Every city and nation has a dominant sound, dominant spirit realm, and a divine destiny.)

- *Repent* for your own sin and corporate sins both past and present.
- *Plead with God* to give grace to the people in the region until they change.
- *Identify the divine destiny* of your city and declare that destiny.
- *Bind the power of the city's strongman* (corporately in partnership with church leaders).
- *Establish a visible presence* in your city so that the people will know where to get the answer.

Freedom of entry to a city is sometimes given to individuals or armies who have given service and protection to the city.

This involves **"the right to enter with swords drawn, bayonets fixed, drums beating, bands playing, colours flying, in full regalia."**

We can stand in the gap and receive conferred authority from God for the spiritual freedom of entry to our city or region.

Chapter 8

Watchmen and Gatekeepers

> To watch means "to lean forward—peer into the distance" (*Hebrew Strong's* 6922).

God tells us not to keep silence and give him no peace till he answers us (Isaiah 62:7). We see the same principle in the New Testament, in Luke 18, the story of the unjust judge who answered the widow because she persisted. God is not unjust, so how much more will he answer; but he has given us the keys to the kingdom, and sometimes we just need to keep praying to overcome demonic resistance, as in the story of Daniel, or for the softening of someone's heart.

God also tells us to keep asking and persisting until we receive what we are praying for. I believe that God will release us from the burden of that prayer when he determines the season is over. Sometimes the answers are not seen or are different to what we requested because God will exercise his divine right to do what is best. It is our responsibility to pray and his to answer however and whenever he sees fit (Matthew 7:7-8).

Gates provide protection from evil and access to what is good.

Jerusalem had seven gates, all with a specific purpose, and there were four thousand gatekeepers in Israel (1 Chronicles 15:23-24, 23:5).

- Sin can come in the gates—Absalom betrayed his father at the gates (2 Samuel 13).
- Gates represent authority—the elders sat in the gates.
- Old Testament cities had both gatekeepers and watchmen (some kept gates and some kept walls).
- God's gates are praise (Isaiah 60:18).

Gates are upheld by pillars.

- The pillars are the values we enforce. They need to be built first. If you destroy the pillar, you destroy both the gate and the building.
- Values are beliefs that direct and change our lives.

If the gates, pillars, or walls are broken down, it brings

- reproach—they are in great trouble and reproach (Nehemiah 1:3).
- grief—the gates are desolate, the priests sigh (Lamentations 1:4).
- attack—Sanballat was angry because they rebuilt the wall (Nehemiah 4).

The Levites (priests) were the Old Testament gatekeepers, but we are now the royal priesthood and therefore hold responsibility to guard specific gates and walls (1 Peter 2:9).

Gates we all guard:

- personal gates (Matthew 15:11, James 3:6)
- eyes, ears, mouth (Psalms 141:3, Exodus 14:14)
- family responsibilities (1 Timothy 5:8)
- spiritual life (1 Corinthians 3:16)
- personal ministry responsibilities (Romans 14:12)

Churches, church movements or denominations, and regional gates are allocated to specific gatekeepers: senior pastors, elders, church leaders, prophets, and apostles.

Church gates are protected through the oversight of the appointed leaders who are supported by the prayer and intercession of the gatekeepers appointed to guard them (Isaiah 62:6, Luke 2:36).

These leaders are the watchmen and see the big picture. Their degree of discernment depends upon their positioning, and because they are placed upon a high place so that they can see the big picture, set upon the walls by God, they can sound an alarm long before the enemy is at the gates. There are also gifted apostles, prophets, and intercessors who can stand on those walls with the church leaders and give greater insight because of their gifting.

The responsibilities of gatekeepers are the following:

- **To guard the presence of God**
  We need to guard the presence of God around our own lives and carry it into our churches so that we guard the presence of God in our services. This can be done by being careful about what input we have into

our lives by what we say and what attitude we bring into the house of God. We should also examine what is in our hearts toward the house and the leaders.

- **Guard temple treasures and storehouses** (values, finances, and doctrine)
  (1 Chronicles 9:17-19, 26:20, 22; Nehemiah 12:25)

- **Prevent what is unclean from entering the temple**
  In the Old Testament, this meant people and animal sacrifices that were classified as unclean; however, now this means unclean practices and fleshly worship or ministry (2 Chronicles 23:19).

- **Gatekeepers need to stay at their posts**
  God told Jeremiah to *stand* in the gates (Jeremiah 7:1).

- **Gatekeepers communicate clearly to the watchmen (senior leaders)**
  The four lepers took the message of freedom to the gatekeepers who took it to the king (2 Kings 7:10-11).

- **Gatekeepers provide the answer (Genesis 37).**
  Joseph not only interpreted Pharaoh's dream but provided the solution.

Empowering and Disempowering Prayer

- Prayer is a help ministry.
- Prayer is a foundation that supports our activities.
- Prayer is a canopy of protection over our city.
- We determine what comes in and out of the gates of our city through prayer.

- Each city has a sound which can be changed through prayer

Prayer is empowered by:

persistence	(Luke 18:1, Ephesians 6:18)
watchfulness	(Matthew 26:41)
waiting	(Isaiah 40:31)
humility	(2 Chronicles 7:14)
wisdom and revelation	(Ephesians 1:15)
unity	(Deuteronomy 32:30)
	(Genesis 11:1-8, Psalm 133)
faith	(Mark 11:24)
praying in the name of Jesus	(John 14:13)

Keys to empowering prayer:

Pray from a position of correct relationship	(Psalms 66:18)
Pray the answer, declaring God's word	(Matthew 17:20)
Pray from a position of authority	(Matthew 16:19, 18:18)
Pray in faith	(Matthew 21:22)
Pray for your specific areas of responsibility	(Matthew 8:9)
Pray patiently and persistently	(Hebrews 10:35-36)
Pray for authorities	(2 Timothy 2:1-8)

Through connection with fivefold ministries, that is, the Ephesians chapter 4 apostles, prophets, pastors, teachers, and evangelists. Prayer supports the fivefold, and the fivefold gives structure and protection to intercessors.

Prayer is disempowered by the following:

- **Sin that is not acknowledged and repented of.**

If I regard iniquity in my heart, the Lord will not hear me (Psalms 66:18).
Why have you not heard? (Isaiah 58:3)
If our hearts do not condemn us, then we have confidence to him (1 John 3:21).
Pride and sin (2 Chronicles 7:14).

- **Unhealthy Relationships**
  God created us for a relationship with him and also with others. We cannot reach our potential or see prayers answered consistently without maintaining our relationships in a healthy way.
  Wives are to obey and honor their husbands, and husbands are to love and understand their wives so that their prayers are not hindered (1 Peter 3:7).
  Reconciliation with other Christians is necessary before we use our gifts (Matthew 5:23).

- **Other hindrances include**
  Unbelief and double-mindedness (James 1:5-8)
  Wrong motives, praying to consume it on your own lusts (James 4:3)
  Disobedience to the word (Proverbs 28:9)
  Demonic interference (Daniel 10:12-14)
  Idolatry worldliness (Ezekiel 14:1-3, Judges 10:11-13)
  Witchcraft prayer (2 Timothy 2:1-8)

When you impose your will over someone else's, you are operating in a form of witchcraft, and this causes confusion in the mind of the person you are praying for. This is also called a soul prayer or a witchcraft prayer. It occurs when you decide what *someone else* should do and pray accordingly.

When you pray for a pastor or church leader,

- identify with their vision and submit your vision to theirs.
- ask them what they would like you to pray for.

Pray for

- God to reveal his will to them (without telling God what his will is).
- health, blessing, and protection over them and their family.
- destruction of the enemy's plans against them.
- cancellation of negative words spoken against them and the prayers of witches or soul prayers of believers or unbelievers.

Scriptural prayers for church leaders:

"Through your prayers I have an abundant supply, that I will not be ashamed and that Christ will be magnified in my body" (Philippians 1:19-20).
"That God would open to us a door" (Colossians 4:2-4).
"That utterance may be given to me, that I may speak boldly and courageously." (Ephesians 6:18-20)

Summary

Pray

- the positive word of God.
- for God to reveal His will to them (without telling God what his will is).

- health, blessing, and protection over them and their family.
- fruitfulness, wisdom, and guidance.
- destruction over the plans of the enemy over them (negative words, etc.).
- God's will over their lives.

God hears all prayer whether spoken out loud or silent. He looks at the intent of our hearts and shows grace to us when we are falling short of his standards. He will not disqualify a sincere prayer, but for consistent answers and increased authority, he has given us guidelines to use.

He gave us a pattern of prayer when the disciples asked him how to pray. He understood that they wanted some guidance because up until then they only knew the prayer they had been taught in the synagogue. It is fine to pray a written prayer as long as your heart is in it and it is not just a habit without meaning, but it is also important to be led by the spirit.

The principles found in the Lord's Prayer show us God's priorities.

Jesus said, "Pray like this." His pattern was to praise God, acknowledge him as a Father, and acknowledge his holiness. Then intercede for his work and for his will to be done in the world. Be kingdom minded and look outside your own needs. When we put others first, we reflect God's nature. Then we can ask for provision of individual daily needs and for his strength in our temptations and troubles.

We pray for God's will to be done, knowing that this happens as we yield to his will in our lives. He has commissioned us to activate his will on earth.

Jesus emphasized that we need to pray daily as he encouraged the disciples to pray for daily provision.

By praying for provision we acknowledge God our Father as our provider. He provides work or financial support through other means on a daily basis and sometimes sends outstanding miracles above and beyond our daily needs.

As we ask for forgiveness and extend forgiveness to others, we release blessing over our lives and break the enemies' plans against us. Jesus taught this graphically in Matthew 18, when he said that the unjust steward who did not forgive the debt owed to him, in spite of receiving such amazing cancellation of debt from his master, would be thrown into prison. Jesus completed his parable with the statement that our Heavenly Father would also let us be thrown into the prison of torment if we did not forgive.

Jesus completes this example of prayer by telling us to pray for deliverance in our testings. Jesus himself is the way of escape when we go through trials and testings.

This prayer is a beautiful pattern for us; it is not limiting what we pray for to these subjects but is a foundation of the prayer we need to maintain.

So we seek and ask, we petition and declare, we praise and worship, and thank God as the spirit leads us.

And God, our loving Heavenly Father, who knows what we need before we ask, hears and answers in the right way and in the right time.

TWENTY-FIRST-CENTURY PROPHET
SECOND EDITION
WORK SHEETS
Part I

Please note: the answers are in your book, usually word for word.

Complete the sentence.

The demonic realm _____ the prophetic child from an early age.

The highest level of the prophet's function can only be achieved through _____.

Part of the enemy's plan is to _____.

Describe one of the distinctives of an emerging prophet that you have seen in your own life. Can you remove this solid line?

How have you been impacted by this? Describe the positives and negatives.

How does God catapult us into the next stage of his plan for us?

What changes does God make in our lives before each new season?

Complete this sentence and describe one instance of this in your life.

Prophets are _____.

*"**Before I formed** you in the womb I knew and approved of you [as my chosen instrument], and before you were born I **separated and set you apart, consecrating you**: [and] I **appointed you** as a prophet to the nations"* (Jeremiah 1:5, Amp).

The word "formed" means to squeeze into shape; it is the same concept used when Jeremiah was told to go down to the potter's house and watch the forming and reshaping of the pot (Jeremiah 18).

Complete these sentences.

The vessel is formed for _____.

Jeremiah was told by God to

Explain the concept of a prophet having no honor in their own country and how the prophet must deal with their feelings about this (John 4:44).

Complete this sentence.

God must purge the prophet of _____.

Every prophet has to contend with the issue of familiarity. What experiences have you had where familiarity created a problem?

In what ways could you have a more constructive response to familiarity?

In what ways does honor open up the prophet's gift?

What caused Elijah to lose his mantle and hand it on to Elisha? (I Kings 19:16)

What does the prophet's pain comes through as described in the chapter of that name?

What spirits commonly manifest against the prophet?

Describe how these spirits have attacked you and how you overcame them.

What two things did David recognize about his battle with Goliath?

Name two activities of the enemies' counterfeit strategy.

Complete these sentences.

We should not seek for _____.

Strong and accurate gifting needs to be married to _____.

What are the signs of a humble and teachable spirit?

What is the first step necessary to transition to the new?

There should always be a redemptive factor in prophecy; the answer should be provided along with any correction

What does the statement "redemptive factor" mean?

Give an example of how you could use could terminology to provide a redemptive factor in a word which speaks of the problem.

Complete this sentence.

The difference between criticism and discernment is
_____

Complete this sentence:

One of the main differences between the gift of prophecy and the office of prophet is the _____ created by a prophet's words.

God asks us to:
_____ the message.
_____ the message.
_____ the message.

What are the two false beliefs that cause the prophet to be unteachable?

I am a prophet _____

A prophet has _____

Consider what could be hindering the fulfillment of your personal prophecies from the teaching "what do I do with my personal prophecy?"

Prepare a strategy to help activate your unfulfilled personal prophecies.

Complete this sentence and name the church leader or ministry leader that you have this type of relationship with.

An accountable relationship is one where _____

What is the role of the person who is called to function as a local church prophet?

What is the pastor's role toward the prophet?

What was the original prophetic promise to women given in Genesis?

Research the scriptures that support this statement:

"The woman is called uniquely by God to make her own decisions about salvation and obedience to him. She is given her own spiritual gifts and calling and will be required by God to give an account of them."

Complete this sentence.

Women changed _____.

Give a definition of false submission.

What did Abigail do to protect vision?

What is the greatest current hindrance to the development of your ministry, and how could you overcome this?

WORK SHEETS
Part II

Describe the difference between a wound and a scar.

Why do we need to be healed of old wounds before we engage in new battles?

An arrow is _____.

What are two wrong foundations in our lives that create a vulnerability to hurt?

_____ based gifting

Explain what each means.

What makes us vulnerable to wounds from the spirit realm?

What strengthens and shapes our personal armor?

In what ways could our lives become "entangled" and hinder our calling?

Describe how this has affected you personally.

Describe the difference between fear and intimidation.

Explain the terms "positional authority" and "experiential authority."

True of false (please tick correct answers).
Generational bondages are overcome by (Tick correct answers and identify one of your personal generational bondages. If you are still finding it difficult, write a strategy to overcome it.)

- Ignoring them
- Applying faith and prayer
- Living in the opposite spirit

Describe *one* of the spiritual outworkings that may be seen in church life when the enemy works through individuals, and outline the strategy that will overcome this.

What do we need to know to determine which spheres of authority we can operate in?

Name the three areas that the army marches on:
1. _____
2. _____
3. _____

What are the three major manifestations of intercession?
1. _____
2. _____
3. _____

Who are the two sources we should communicate to in battle?
1. _____
2. _____

Describe the three classifications of spirits that we need to identify so that we war in a safe way, using the level of authority that we are commissioned for.

What are the three keys to using authority?
1. _____
2. _____
3. _____

What are the three levels of authority?
1. _____
2. _____
3. _____

What type of authority is delegated to us in the following scriptures?

Luke 9:1
Matt 16:19
Luke 10:19

Choose one aspect of disempowering prayer, and give an example of how that could occur in your own life.

Describe the term "witchcraft prayer."

Give two examples of a godly way to pray for your pastor.

Using the scripture Romans 8:6, explain what a "carnal" weapon is.

Complete the sentence.

"Authority without relationship and accountability becomes _____ an _____."

Ephesians 4:1-16 talks about unity in the church.
What attributes help us to walk in unity?
What is the fruit of walking in unity?

Prophetic Activations

These activations will help your prophetic gift to grow. Ask God to show you other ways to practice your gift.

Boundaries of the prophetic gift (1 Corinthians 14:3)

- Comfort
- Edification
- Encouragement

Wise terminology

- "This may mean something to you."
- "How does this sit with you?"
- "I may be wrong, but what do you think about this?"
- "I'm not sure, but I keep feeling this thing."
- "While I was praying, I thought this word could be referring to you."

Processing Prophetic Words

1. Receive the message.
2. Receive the authority to deliver it.
3. Let the Holy Spirit interpret it.

How Prophecy Comes
Many words—may start with our spirit feeling stirred.
We may hear or see words or pictures.
The complete message will form as you stay focused.

The sense of a message will come.
Ask God for the words. Start by faith.

Pictures
Ask the Holy Spirit for words to express it.
If they don't come then share the picture without explanation.
Pictures can be the start of a prophecy.

Songs—either a song you know or a song of the spirit.
A song you know is not necessarily meant to be sung; it may be a memory trigger.
Wait on God for the words.

Scriptures—a *rhema* word (**John 14:26**)
This is a revealed portion of the word of God, a specific word for a specific person or people at a specific time and circumstance.
You may just give the scripture or it may be the start of a prophecy.
Prophecy is always, in part, progressive and conditional.

Stage One
Select a partner (someone you don't know well), and give them *one word* only. Ask for feedback on its accuracy.
Ask God to give you *more details*.
These details are received through questioning:
"What else do you want to say to them God?"

Areas that God may want to speak on include:

- specific emotional needs.
- commendation for what they have done.
- God's provision.
- their gifting and calling (don't move out of your boundaries and faith level here).

Stage Two

Ask God to give you a *scripture* for your partner. You don't necessarily need to know the reference. Don't seek to explain or interpret it.

Ask them for feedback on its accuracy.

Rate yourself: POOR / FAIR / GREAT / EXCELLENT

Stage Three

In a group of three or four, give *one* person a simple prophecy.

Give *each* person a simple prophecy.

Ask God for more details about your last prophecy.

Hot Tip!

Listen for a "quickened" word in the prophecy, the word that seems to have a lot of emphasis on it, and pray for more detail on that word or subject.

Rate yourself: POOR / FAIR / GREAT / EXCELLENT

Stage Four

Choose a psalm or another passage of scripture that you are not familiar with, and ask God for a *rhema* word or fresh revelation on it. Write it down.

Ask God who the revelation is for and give it to them.

Ask for their feedback.

Write down a personal word for yourself.

Have your partner write a word for you and compare them.

Pray for a word of knowledge for someone in a group.
Minister the answer to them.

Pray for a word of knowledge for a *specific person*.
Minister the answer to them.

Pray for a *specific* word of knowledge for someone in a group.
Minister the answer to them.

Rate yourself: POOR / FAIR / GREAT / EXCELLENT

Stage Five

Give a *specific* word to your partner on a subject they choose: finances, family, ministry, etc. Ask for their feedback.

Give a *specific* word to *three or more* people, one after another, on a subject they have chosen and receive their feedback.

Prophesy a brief word to each person in the row. Start immediately and keep the prophecy short. The aim of this activation is to learn to hear from God quickly.

Rate yourself: POOR / FAIR / GREAT / EXCELLENT

Stage Six

Write down a *general* word for someone whose name is on a piece of paper, without seeing their name.
Write down a *specific* word for someone whose name is on a piece of paper, without seeing their name.
You ask God for the area He wants to speak to them about.

Prophesy blindfolded to an *unknown person*.

Prophesy blindfolded to *several people, one after another*.

Prophesy blindfolded to one person on *their chosen subject*.

Prophesy blindfolded to *several people*, one after another on *their chosen subject*.

Prophesy blindfolded to *one person* on the subject God speaks *to you* about.

Prophesy to an *unknown person* on a recording device

Receive feedback from the friend or relative of the person who submitted the name.

Preach from *scripture* given to you with no time to prepare.

Preach from an *object* given to you with no time to prepare.

Rate yourself: POOR / FAIR / GREAT / EXCELLENT

Stage Seven

From the front of a group, select the person God wants to speak to and prophesy to them.

Prophesy for set periods of time—three minutes, five minutes, seven minutes—on a given subject, achieving 50 percent or more accuracy as far as can be determined.

Hot Tips!
Remember that medical doctors take an oath, which starts with the promise "first do no harm." When you operate in the prophetic, you are a spiritual doctor. "First do no harm."

- Ask God to show you creative ways to practice your gift without risking harm to anybody
- Ask others who are more experienced in the prophetic than you to evaluate your gift operations.

> **ALL THESE STEPS CAN BE REPEATED AGAIN AND AGAIN BECAUSE THE GIFT IS DEVELOPED THROUGH REPEATED PRACTICE!**

Printed in Great Britain
by Amazon.co.uk, Ltd.,
Marston Gate.